The hm Learning and Study Skills Program

Student Text Level I

Fourth Edition

Edited by Judy Tilton Brunner and Matthew S. Hudson, EdD

ROWMAN & LITTLEFIELD
Lanham • Boulder • New York • London

Published by Rowman & Littlefield
A wholly owned subsidiary of The Rowman & Littlefield Publishing Group, Inc.
4501 Forbes Boulevard, Suite 200, Lanham, Maryland 20706
www.rowman.com

16 Carlisle Street, London W1D 3BT, United Kingdom

British Library Cataloguing in Publication Information Available

Library of Congress Cataloging-in-Publication Data Available
ISBN 978-1-4758-0383-9 (pbk. : alk. paper)—978-1-4758-0384-6 (electronic)

∞™ The paper used in this publication meets the minimum requirements of American National Standard for Information Sciences—Permanence of Paper for Printed Library Materials, ANSI/NISO Z39.48-1992.

Printed in the United States of America

CONTENTS

INTRODUCTION TO THE *hm* LEARNING
AND STUDY SKILLS PROGRAM: LEVEL I

How Do You Learn?

Not everyone learns in the same way. Some people like to read about something new before they try it. Other people like to learn when they can actually "do" whatever they are learning. Some want to be able to imagine how to do something before they try it. Still others like to be told about a new thing. They like to discuss it before they try to do it. Can you think of any other ways that people learn to do new things?

What is your preference?

Exercise I

Directions: What do you do well? Look at the list below, and pick *one* thing that you feel you have learned to do well. Or if you prefer, pick your own activity. Write your choice on the space provided. Be sure to pick something you remember learning.

read	cook	debate
write	play a sport	use a word processor
sail	ride a bike	play a computer game
ski	find Internet information	knit
play an instrument	draw	care for an animal
sew	ice-skate	solve math problems

Exercise II

Directions: Think about the thing you learned to do very well. How did you learn to do it?

watching	listening	doing
reading	thinking about	working when I have to
experimenting	writing	getting it right
learning from my mistakes	proving my point	"hands on"
being creative	talking it over	with a group
with a friend	by myself	asking questions
doing something I care about	looking things up	get a feeling that it's right
practice		

Look at the words and phrases listed. Circle the ones that describe how you learn best. You may also write other words and phrases that describe how you learn in the space provided.

_____

_____

_____

_____

_____

_____

Remember: There are no right or wrong answers! You can circle and write as many words and phrases as you need to describe how you learn.

Exercise III

Directions: Look again at the list in Exercise I. This time pick out something that you have had *trouble* trying to learn well. Or if you prefer, pick your own activity. Write your choice on the lines that follow.

_____

_____

_____

1. How did you try to learn the thing you said you had *trouble* learning? Look at the list in Exercise II again. Pick some ways that you tried to learn, and write these ways in the space provided.

_____

_____

_____

_____

2. Have you chosen any different ways than you chose for Exercise II? _____

If you answered "yes," write the different ways in the space provided.

_____

_____

_____

_____

What Are Learning and Study Skills?

Learning and study skills are *ways or methods for learning.* They are ways of doing what you are asked to do in school that can help you to learn better. When you use learning and study skills, you can often get more done in a given period of time and learn more, too.

Some examples of learning and study skills are these: active listening, tuning into directions, reading for meaning, taking notes, solving problems, and preparing for tests.

How Do You Learn Study and Learning Skills?

People learn study and learning skills through practice. You don't learn how to play basketball or use a keyboard by talking about it. You have to play it. The same is true with learning and study skills.

You often learn study and learning skills best through the mistakes you make. Everyone makes mistakes. What's important is that you look at your mistakes carefully and find out what caused them. When you know what caused a particular mistake, you'll know how not to make that mistake again.

Why Are Learning and Study Skills Important?

Learning will not suddenly become simple just because you have learned to use learning and study skills. But these skills will help you to become a better learner. You will probably find school more rewarding and enjoyable. You will also be more able to learn whatever you want outside of school.

Directions for the Study Skills Pretest

Before beginning this program, complete the survey that follows. Be honest with your answers.

Study Skills Survey

	Always	Sometimes	Never
I review my assignments every day.			
I try to study in a quiet place.			
When necessary, I ask for help.			
I keep a folder for each subject.			
I keep my folders organized.			
I write sample test questions and answer the questions.			
I do my homework as early in the day as possible.			
I keep a "to-do" list of assignments.			
I turn in all assignments on time.			
When I take notes, I always write a summary from my notes of what I learned.			
I begin studying for tests several days in advance of the exam.			
I compare my notes to a classmate's notes.			
I take written notes over text material.			
I look at bold print, italics, the writing in margins, and study questions before I begin a reading assignment.			
I ask the teacher to explain things when I'm confused.			
When learning new information, I read the text slowly.			
When I have several homework assignments, I finish the hardest ones first.			
When I sit down to study, I have all my supplies organized and ready to use—paper, pencils, computer, etc.			

WAYS TO LISTEN

Listening Is More Than Just Hearing

The average student spends more than half of each school day *listening*. That means that you give more time to listening than to anything else you do in school.

Most people think of listening as something as natural as walking or eating. They don't think of it as anything you have to work at to do well. But we are not *born* good listeners. We learn to be good listeners.

Why is this so? Hearing is a natural ability, but *listening* is more than just hearing. Listening means directing your attention to—or *focusing on*—what you're hearing and trying to make sense of what you've heard.

Listening is a study skill. It's one of the most important study skills because listening is a part of almost everything else that you do. It seems simple, but it's not. Being a good listener doesn't come naturally. It requires learning and practice.

Why Is It Hard to Listen Even When Interested?

Generally people talk at a rate of about 125 words per minute. However, we think at a speed that is more than three times as fast, about 400 words per minute. That means our thoughts move much faster than the words we hear. So it's not surprising that we often let our attention wander away from what another person is saying to us.

The key to becoming a good listener is to be an *active* listener: to keep your thoughts *focused* on what is heard.

The Listening Game

Directions: A story will be read aloud to you only *once*. Pay close attention to the details of the story. When the story is finished, you will be asked to tell what you have heard. Listen carefully! (You are not allowed to take notes.)

Steps in Active Listening

It is a *fact* that we can all become active listeners. So remember the word *fact*. It will help you remember the steps in *active listening*, because the first letter of each of the steps spells the word *FACT*.

Step 1: **F**ocus

The first step in active listening is to *focus*. This means to give your attention to something. Television often "catches" your attention. It doesn't require you to do the active work of *focusing*. However, when your father calls you from the next room as you are watching television, you have to pull your mind from the television to really focus on what he is saying.

Step 2: **A**sk

While you listen, *ask* yourself questions about what the speaker is saying. Then try to answer your questions, or see if the speaker answers them. Asking and answering questions in this way can help you make sense of the speaker's message.

When you are listening in school, you might *ask* yourself: What is it that the teacher wants me to know? Do I understand this? What don't I understand about what I am hearing? Does this make sense to me?

Step 3: **C**onnect

Keep asking yourself why the speaker is saying what she or he is saying. Try to *connect* the main ideas with each other. For instance, the speaker may talk about growing food in a certain place. You already know that these things are needed for people to grow food: climate, soil conditions, and technology. As the speaker is talking, you will listen for and *connect* the main ideas of climate, soil conditions, and technology in order to understand how the food is grown.

Step 4: **T**ry to Picture

Try to picture in your mind what the speaker is saying. Some people find that they can listen and remember better if they use their imaginations to make *mind pictures*. For example, if you are listening to a set of directions about how to get somewhere, make an imaginary map of the directions in your mind.

Try It Again: The Listening Game

Directions: Again a story will be read to you only *once*. Try out the *steps in active listening*. *Focus* on the speaker so you can pay close attention to the details of the story. *Ask* yourself how these details *connect*. *Try to picture* what is happening.

When the story is finished, you will be asked to tell what you have heard.

1. Did you find listening any easier this time? _____ If so, why?

    _____

    _____

    _____

    _____

2. Which of the *steps in active listening* is the most difficult for you to do?

_____

_____

_____

_____

3. Why do you think this is so?

_____

_____

_____

_____

Unit I Summary

We are not born as good listeners. We have to learn to listen well. Active listening is a study skill.

We can learn to listen actively by following these steps:

Focus: Look at the speaker. Try to pay attention to what is being said.

Ask questions: Try to figure out what is important by asking questions. Then answer your questions, or see if the speaker answers your questions.

Connect: "Make sense" out of what the speaker is saying by *connecting* main ideas with each other.

Try to picture: Try to see "in your mind's eye" what the speaker is talking about.

Technology Adaptation

- Listen to a podcast and write a summary of what was learned.

- Listen to a program on National Public Radio. Take notes during the program and compare the notes to a classmate's notes.

- Listen to a chapter of an audio book. Draw a picture of what was learned.

UNIT II
TUNING INTO DIRECTIONS

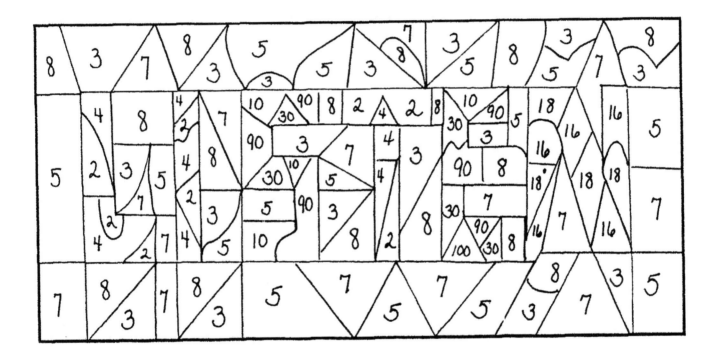

Exercise I

You will find that listening to and following directions is a very important skill. This is true not only in schoolwork but also in your daily life. Probably each of you has a story about a time when you only half heard or didn't hear a direction. Afterward you found yourself in a complete mess, like the man in the old joke:

He thought they said "trains" when they passed out brains, so he ran to catch one.

Never got himself a brain!

It seems that the man in the joke shares a problem with many people. Some students in a midwestern school received very poor grades on an achievement test. When they investigated the cause of these results, guidance counselors and classroom teachers found not poor students but poor listeners. These students had never before taken this kind of test. They weren't tuned in to listening to and following directions. So they could only guess at what they were supposed to do.

You can't guess about directions and expect to be right! You need to listen carefully and ask questions if you don't understand what you have heard.

You are already showing that you are a good listener because you are reading this page as you were instructed. Now here's an important clue! You must listen to and follow only directions number 3, 7, and 9 the next time your teacher reads the directions.

The students in the Midwestern school were then taught how to listen to directions. They also learned to read directions more carefully. When they took the achievement test again, they did much better. After you have read this page carefully, keep the secret to yourself! Write 3, 7, and 9 on the page before this one so you will know what directions to follow. Listen carefully, follow the right directions, and you will spell the right word in crayon.

Unit II Summary

Remember the steps in active listening from Unit I. They are these:

Focus: Look at the speaker. Try to pay attention to what is being said.

Ask questions: Try to figure out what is important by asking questions. Then answer your questions, or see if the speaker answers your questions.

Connect: *Make sense* out of what the speaker is saying by *connecting* main ideas with each other.

Try to picture: Try to see *in your mind's eye* what the speaker is saying.

Reading and listening to directions is an important skill. This is true not only in school but in any situation in life.

Always read directions carefully. Be sure to read *all* of the directions. Then if you don't understand, ask questions. If you are not allowed to ask questions, ask yourself the questions and listen for the answers.

Listen carefully when someone is giving you directions. Don't try to guess what they are. Listen to *all* of the directions. Then if you don't understand what you've heard, ask questions.

If you can't remember all the directions, write them down on a piece of paper.

Technology Adaptation

- Age Calculation

    1. Multiply the first number of the age by 5. (If < 10—e.g., 5—consider it as 05. If it is > 100—e.g., 102—then take 10 as the first digit, 2 as the second one.)

    2. Add 3.

    3. Multiply by 2.

4. Add the second digit of the age.

5. Subtract 6.

6. Ask students to read what is on their screens. (The answer should come out as the user's age.)

- Always 73

    1. Choose a four-digit number and enter it twice. (e.g., 4356 would be entered 43564356.) Make sure the students remember the original four-digit number.

    2. Divide by 137.

    3. Divide by the original four-digit number.

    4. The answer will always be 73, no matter what four-digit combination they choose (except for 0000 of course).

UNIT III
GETTING THE TIMING DOWN

Introduction

When you read or hear a story, you can understand it better if you know the order in which the events are taking place. Knowing the order of events means that you know what happened first, what happened next, and so on.

Another way of saying this is that you know the *sequence* of events.

"Getting the timing down" means to understand the sequence of events in a story. Sequencing may include putting events in order (chronological), writing steps in order (e.g., instructions, recipes), and organizing a passage of text to improve understanding.

The exercises in this unit will help you learn more about "getting the timing down" or *sequencing*.

Exercise I: Philip's Story—What's the Sequence of Events?

Directions: Read the paragraphs that follow, and complete all italicized instructions.

Refer to the map of Philip's neighborhood. Philip lives in the last house on the right side of Torrey Avenue as you are heading west. *Mark his house so you can see where he lives.*

Philip has many errands to do, and he only has a short time before he has to pick up his sister, Anne, at the day care center.

You will see a list of Philip's errands. *First read over all of the errands.* You can use your map as a reference as you read them. *Then figure out in what sequence Philip should do his errands so he can do them as quickly as possible.* Marking the map in pencil may be helpful to you.

When you have decided on a sequence, number the errands so they will show the sequence of events. In the space on the left of each errand, mark the first errand #1, the second #2, and so on.

A. _____ Philip is hungry. He buys a double scoop pistachio and chocolate ice cream cone at CHUCK'S.

B. _____ Philip wants to see *The Hunger Games*, which is playing at the THEATER tonight. He stops to buy two tickets.

13

C. _____ Philip takes his little sister, Anne, to DONNA'S KENNELS to look at the puppies.

D. _____ Philip decides to ride his bike so he can do everything faster. The tires need air. Before he can do anything else, he goes to F.B. GARAGE to fill his tires.

E. _____ Philip brings Anne home. He listens to music and relaxes. It's been a long afternoon, but it's all over now.

F. _____ Philip wants to play baseball this year, so he stops to register at WELLINGTON FIELD. He notices the theater's billboard across the street.

G. _____ Philip has to pick up his little sister, Anne, at C.T.'s DAYCARE. Anne begs to see the puppies at DONNA'S KENNELS.

H. _____ Philip drops two overdue books off at the LIBRARY. He doesn't go in to pay for them because he still has ice cream on his hands.

I. _____ DORIE'S COOKIE FACTORY sells day-old cookies at half price. Philip's mother wants him to pick up a pound of cookies, so he does.

PHILIP'S NEIGHBORHOOD

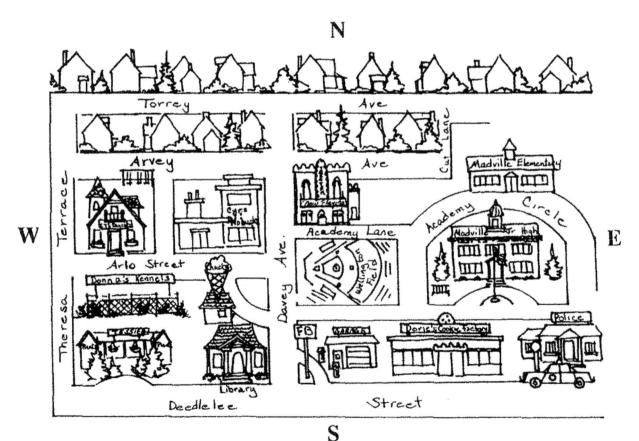

Key Words: Time Qualifiers

When you read or listen to a story, you will often find key words that can give you an idea about *when* events in the story take place. These key words are *time qualifiers*. These words qualify other words or phrases. To qualify is to make the meaning of words or phrases clearer.

Some examples of *time qualifiers* that tell you more about when events take place are these:

while	during	before
after	as	until
following	afterward	in the meantime

There are many other *time qualifiers*. Any word or phrase that helps you to understand when events are happening is a *time qualifier*.

Exercise II

Directions: Each of the sentences that follow includes two events. In each sentence, circle the word(s) that you recognize as a *time qualifier*. Then underline the event that happens first. If the events in a sentence are happening at the same time, do not underline anything.

Example

Before Molly left for school, she ate two pieces of toast. We set up the tents while the others gathered firewood. I had a great time after I got to know all of the people there.

1. Before Miguel had realized the danger he was in, he enjoyed sailing over the wild waves.

2. Amanda searched for clues to the disappearance of her brother, Cody, but in the meantime, he slept soundly, unaware that she was trying to find him.

3. It had taken years of hard work, but finally the statue was finished.

4. Following the wedding ceremony, there was a reception at the Martin Luther King Community Center.

5. Water expands when it is cooled.

6. As the ice masses drew back, they carved lakes and hills on the earth's surface.

7. Divide the money equally among yourselves, and then go to the store.

8. All during the time I had been outdoors planting, the baby had been playing happily in her pen.

9. The water pressure built up until the dam finally cracked.

15

Finding Clues to the Timing

Sometimes the events described in a story are not in a sequence. The author may tell one part of the story and then jump into the past or the future. When an author jumps around in time like this, she or he must give clues to help the reader understand what is happening. Often these clues are *time qualifiers*.

When you are reading or listening to a story, pay attention to the *time qualifiers*. They can help you understand what happened and when it happened. This helps you to follow the story better.

Exercise III

Directions: While reading the story, pay close attention to the time qualifiers. Underline each time qualifier. Then number the events listed in the order in which they happened. Number the first event #1, the second event #2, and so on.

The skies were heavy with thick, gray clouds. It was only three o'clock. Still early, Nick thought, so he'd have plenty of time to get home. Earlier this morning Nick had listened to the weather report. The weather people had predicted a major snowstorm. From the looks of the sky, he was sure that the prediction would come true.

Nick was excited. He loved the snow. The prospect of walking home in the snowstorm did not bother him at all. He was well bundled and had just a little less than a mile to go. The path through the woods was completely clear. If it did snow, it would be the first snow of the season.

After Nick had been walking for about ten minutes, thick flakes began to swirl around him. Long ago, when he was in preschool, his teacher had told the class that each flake that fell from the sky was different. Ever since then, Nick had tried to find two flakes that were exactly alike. He hadn't found them yet, but he was sure that of the millions that fell from the sky, if he kept looking, he would find the magical pair. He'd always told himself that when he found them, he would get whatever he'd wish for.

Nick was so busy catching and examining the lovely flakes that he didn't notice that the storm was intensifying. The swirling flakes had gathered force. The forest path was now a line of white winding through the tall pines. But Nick was not concentrating on the gathering forces of the snow. He was mesmerized by the thought of finding the two identical flakes. He stopped in his favorite spot, a clearing beneath two sycamore trees, so that he would have more light to examine the snow.

By the time he gave some attention to what was happening around him, the snow had become thick. It was so thick, in fact, that he could barely make out the outline of the trees around the clearing. He became a bit alarmed as he remembered his mother telling him, "Nick, this will be our first winter here. The storms in these parts come up quickly. You don't get the same warning as we did back east. Soon the ground is covered, and you can't see your hand in front of your face."

At the time Nick thought his mother was being a bit overly cautious. Not even here in the Midwest could a storm sneak up that quickly on a boy who had experienced snowstorms all his life. But as Nick searched for the path that should now continue through a grove of maples, he knew his mother had been right to warn him.

Still, he wasn't worried. He was very close to home, after all, and the snow was just beginning to cover the ground. He did, however, quicken his pace. In his haste and because the snow made the forest a new, strange world, Nick took the wrong turn. He had gone half a mile when he discovered that he was heading toward the pond, not the old farmhouse that his family had moved into last summer.

The storm was lashing out in all its fury. Nick couldn't see the nose in front of his face, much less his hand. The maple and ash trees no longer protected the winding path. Now Nick was worried. He raced in what he thought was the right direction. It was getting dark. Soon he would not even have the comfort of daylight.

"Whatever am I going to do?" thought Nick as he admitted to himself that he didn't know if he was heading home or in some wild circle toward the pond. He was growing tired, and he realized that he'd have to catch his breath and think clearly before going on. He pulled his coat away from his watch to see how much time he would have left before total darkness was upon him. Instead of looking at his watch, he saw, wide-eyed, two snowflakes that for all the world looked perfectly alike. Here was the chance to test his theory.

"Oh, I wish I could find my way home!"

Just then, his dog, Buddy, bounded into his arms. He was a great German shepherd with an amazing sense of direction. Nick knew now he had found his way home.

Number each sentence in the order it occurred in the story.

a. _____ Nick's family moved from the East.

b. _____ The weather people had predicted a snowstorm.

c. _____ Nick's mother had warned him about midwestern snowstorms.

d. _____ Nick's preschool teacher had told him no two snowflakes were alike.

e. _____ The storm was intensifying.

f. _____ Nick noticed the powerful storm.

g. _____ Nick was looking for a pair of identical snowflakes.

h. _____ It was three o'clock in the afternoon.

i. _____ Nick's dog, Buddy, found him.

j. _____ Nick had taken the wrong turn.

Predicting Outcomes

When you are reading or listening to a story, you can use *time qualifiers* to help you understand the sequence of events. Then when you know what has already happened, you can often figure out what will happen next in the story.

Figuring out what will probably happen next is called *predicting outcomes*. When you predict an outcome, you use what you already know about a story to make a "good guess" about what will happen next.

Trying to *predict outcomes* also helps you to become actively involved in whatever you're hearing or reading.

When you predict an outcome, you ask yourself questions and try to answer them before you read or are told what happens.

Exercise IV

Directions: Read the following paragraphs. Underline the *time qualifiers* that help you to think about the possible outcome of each story. Then answer the question that follows each paragraph.

1. When I awoke this morning, the sun was shining brightly in a clear, blue sky. I was excited because this was the day I had planned for the big picnic. After breakfast I turned on the radio and heard the weather report: "A moist cold front will be traveling rapidly across the Pacific Northwest. This front will push out the high currently settled over our region and will bring heavy rain. Rains will continue into tomorrow." When I looked at the mountain to the west, I saw billowing, black clouds.

   Do you think this person will have a picnic on this day? What makes you think this?

   _____

   _____

   _____

   _____

   _____

2. My teacher asked me to do an experiment to prove that a vacuum, or empty space, can't exist if there is something available to fill it. I knew that a candle needed oxygen to burn, and I also knew that oxygen took up space. So I put a candle in a shallow bowl and put an inch of water into the bowl. When I put a glass jar over the candle, I knew the candle would go out after it had used up all the oxygen within the jar. Then, with all the oxygen gone, the empty space within the jar would need to be filled, if possible, with another substance.

   Predict what will happen to the water in the bowl. Explain your prediction.

   _____

   _____

   _____

   _____

   _____

3. They say that if you don't learn from your mistakes, then "history will repeat itself." I never knew what that meant until I figured out there was a reason why I kept turning up on the "lost list." The first time I got lost, I had an excuse: I was only five years old. My mother had said, "Stay right here while Mama tries this dress on." I didn't listen to her. Instead I followed a cart full of toys. I should have learned to listen from that experience, but I didn't. I was seven when the teacher told our class to report to the auditorium after lunch. Again I wasn't listening, so I spent the better part of the afternoon looking for my class. When it finally came time for our class trip to Montreal, I was really excited. I was also determined not to get lost, but as I said, "History has a way of repeating itself."

Do you think the writer gets lost in Montreal? Why do you think the way you do?

_____

_____

_____

_____

_____

4. In 1641 the population of New France was 240. Most of the people living there were single soldiers. French officials asked unmarried women to come to the New World to become soldiers' wives. Ships soon arrived in New France carrying more than 150 female immigrants. Then the government offered special rewards for large families. If people had ten children, they received a pension. Girls were given large sums if they married before they were sixteen. Boys who married before the age of twenty also received special rewards.

Predict the population of New France in 1675. What makes you think this?

_____

_____

_____

_____

_____

Unit III Summary

"Getting the timing down" means understanding the order of events in a story. The order in which things take place in a story is also called the *sequence* of events.

When you read or listen to a story, you can recognize key words that tell you about when events take place. These words are called *time qualifiers*. Some examples of time qualifiers are these: *after, before, until, while, following, during.*

You can use your ability to "get the timing down" to understand when things happen in a story and to *predict outcomes*. This means to use what you already know about the sequence of events in a story to figure out what will probably happen next. By trying to predict outcomes when reading or listening, readers are more active and involved.

Technology Adaptation

- Develop a timeline of major events in your life.

    1. When were you born?

    2. What school did you attend first and when?

    3. Have you ever won anything, placed in an event, or received a trophy or ribbon?

- These are just examples. The timeline will be about you.

- Use a program like SmartArt in Microsoft Office or search "timeline maker" on the Internet to use a free program.

- Search for a recipe online. Copy and paste a recipe you found for "homemade yeast rolls" into a word-processing program. Rearrange the order of directions and explain why changing the order might make a difference in the outcome of the finished bread.

Books Involving Timing Sequence

Goldilocks and the Three Bears

The Three Little Pigs

Seven Blind Mice

The Wizard of Oz

UNIT IV
A MATTER OF TIME

Introduction

Think about the meaning of the word *time*. Can you give a definition for this word? Does this word have more than one meaning for you?

Write your definition for the word *time* on the lines below. If you can think of more than one definition, write two or three.

time: _____

_____

_____

_____

_____

_____

You may have found it difficult to define the word *time*. Time is not something we can touch, see, or smell. Yet we can "feel" time or sense it as it passes. And we can also "hear" time or sense the order in a piece of music.

Our sense of time seems to change as we grow older. For instance, when we are younger, time seems to pass by slowly like when playing with friends or doing something fun. As we get older, time in school, for example, seems to pass slowly and free time seems to pass by more quickly. Think about the last time you took a nap—the time probably went by faster than you wanted it to! Then imagine the amount of time you needed, but maybe did not spend, when studying for your last test at school. With proper planning, you can use time and time management with tools like a calendar or agenda to provide you ample time for all activities. This unit will help you to look more carefully at what time is, how you use your time, and how to plan.

Exercise I

Directions: Read the directions and then complete the time log using a pencil. Total the number of hours and minutes spent in a typical day. Your total should be approximately 24 hours (1 day).

How do you spend your time? You may not remember everything you do in the course of the day, but there are 24 hours for everyone! Some events are routine and occur daily or weekly, while some events are special and only occur occasionally. Some events happen in just a few minutes while others can take several hours. On the following log, reflect and make a good guess about how much time you spend each day on each activity. It is a list of suggested activities only. You may want to personalize this list to your own needs. Assign a time (hours or minutes) to the list using the blank space provided for each activity listed. On the blank lines (at the bottom of the suggested list), add your own personal activities specific to you. Cross out anything that does not apply to you. There are no right or wrong answers.

Time Spent	Activity
_____	Get ready in the morning
_____	Eat breakfast
_____	Feed/water pets
_____	Attend school
_____	Eat lunch
_____	Participate in sports/clubs
_____	Do homework
_____	Eat dinner
_____	Text friends
_____	Read
_____	Spend time with friends
_____	Listen to music
_____	Clean your room
_____	Watch TV
_____	Play a video game
_____	Sleep
_____	_____
_____	_____
_____	_____
_____	TOTAL TIME (should be approximately 24 hours)

Now, be more specific and specify the amount of time you spend on each subject during the school day. List the name for the subject/class and the amount of time you spend there.

<u>Time Spent</u>   <u>Subject Name/Class</u>

_____   _____

_____   _____

_____   _____

_____   _____

_____   _____

_____   _____

_____   _____

_____   _____

_____   TOTAL TIME

A String of Events—Planning the Steps

When you have a certain project in mind such as making a craft, assembling something, or getting a book report ready for school, you often think through the things you need to do—or steps you need to take to complete the project. What's the first step? The second one? And so on.

For instance, if you want to do your book report, you think about all the things that need to be done before you can write a final draft. Some of those things might be:

- read the book

- discuss the book with your teacher

- outline the main events

- outline the main characters

- write a rough draft

You must have a clear idea of the project you wish to do. You must also think of the steps you need to take in order to get this project done. It is helpful to think of these steps as a string of events. In other words, all the steps you take and the order in which you take them must have a logical connection. You cannot outline the main events of the book until you have read the book.

Exercise II

Directions: Look at the example and events 1–2. The steps that are listed below each number are not in the correct order.

Suggest a better order by numbering the first thing to be done as #1, and the second thing as #2, and so on.

Example: Make pancakes

    a. _____   mix ingredients

    b. _____   heat skillet

    c. _____   read recipe

    d. _____   eat pancakes

    e. _____   find recipe

    f. _____   get out necessary ingredients

    g. _____   put mixture in hot, greased skillet

    h. _____   flip pancakes

Event # 1—Pick out a birthday present

    a. _____   wrap the present

    b. _____   check to see if I have enough money to buy the present

    c. _____   give the present to my friend

    d. _____   go shopping

    e. _____   find out what my friend wants/needs

    f. _____   attend the birthday party

Event # 2—Plan to see a movie

    a. _____   text or call my friend

    b. _____   check available movies online or use a movie/show app

    c. _____   suggest going to a movie together

d. _____ check to see if I have enough money

e. _____ get permission from parents

f. _____ arrange a ride to the movie

Event # 3—Setting goals using time helps motivate you to get something done, especially those tasks you may not want to do. As you work on schoolwork, for example, set goals where you can reward yourself when something is accomplished. For this example, we will use your daily homework. Let's assume you have an average of one hour of homework each weeknight. Using the list from Exercise I, list the top five activities you enjoy doing the most:

Time Spent   Activity

_____   _____

_____   _____

_____   _____

_____   _____

_____   _____

Now, we are going to balance what you like to do with your homework time. For the purposes of this exercise, we are going to start your free time after school ends for the day until your usual bedtime. In the space provided list how many hours (average) you have each day from the time school ends to the time you go to bed.

_____

_____

_____

This time you have remaining time to decide how you want to spend it. Assuming you have one hour of time for homework each night, how can you adjust your desired activities to account for this? On the list below, reorganize your time allowed for each activity allowing for one hour of homework time.

Time Spent   Activity

_____   _____

_____   _____

_____   _____

_____   _____

_____   _____

Exercise III

Directions: Using a weekly calendar, record your class each day by subject for one week. It is strongly encouraged for you to record *all* events that take 10 minutes or longer in your day including chores, activities, and so on. Practice completing your agenda or log by starting on the current day.

WEEKLY CALENDAR

Monday, [Day]	
Tuesday, [Day]	
Wednesday, [Day]	
Thursday, [Day]	
Friday, [Day]	
Saturday, [Day]	
Sunday, [Day]	

Using Your Agenda/Time Log: What Happened?

How did you spend your time this past week? After reviewing your results, you may be surprised how you spent your time. Think about the questions below and then answer them honestly.

1. Did anything get in the way of my schedule? (If things did get in the way, what were they?)

   _____

   _____

   _____

   _____

2. Did I get everything done that I wanted to do?

   _____

   _____

   _____

   _____

3. What did I spend the most time doing this past week?

   _____

   _____

   _____

   _____

4. How could I make better use of my time?

   _____

   _____

   _____

   _____

5. How does using this agenda/time log seem helpful to me?

   _____

   _____

   _____

   _____

6. What was not helpful from these exercises and why?

_____

_____

_____

_____

Unit IV Summary

- Keeping an agenda or time log will help you get organized with your time.

- Specifically, this unit provided tools to help you identify how you spend your time, how to plan, and how to set time goals for things you have to do and for things you want to do.

- Time is a delicate act of balancing since there are only 24 hours in each day. Recording daily events (including school subjects/assignments) in an agenda or time log provides a detailed record of how you spend your day. This exercise allows you to determine what adjustments might be needed to ensure you are maximizing time on task. This will allow you more time to do the fun things you enjoy.

- Keeping this daily log also creates a good habit you will hopefully continue in the future.

Technology Adaptation

- Use an online calendar program to keep track of your daily log.

- If you have a smart phone or other device available, investigate free apps about time management and scheduling. Keep a daily log of entries on how you spend your time each day.

- Use an electronic calendar program using your device to keep track of your day.

UNIT V
PUTTING IDEAS TOGETHER

Introduction

Putting ideas together by categorization is an important foundation skill. First, you need to learn to recognize the interrelatedness of detail. When information is categorized, it is easier to remember.

This unit will give you practice with categorization. It will also help you remember information more effectively.

Exercise 1

Directions: Look at the words in group A. Then answer the questions below the list. List the letters of phrases or sentences that you choose. You do not need to copy the phrase or sentence itself. Do the same for group B.

Group A

a. go to the store

b. return a book to the library

c. take out the trash

d. pick up laundry

e. text Sarah

f. play a video game

1. Which phrase(s) fit into the category of chores? _____

_____

_____

_____

2. Which phrase(s) fit into the category of errands? _____

_____

_____

_____

3. Which phrase(s) fit into the category of things to do in my free time?_____

_____

_____

_____

4. Name a category in which all of these phrases fit. _____

_____

_____

_____

Group B

   a. examining animal characteristics and behavior

   b. analyzing data gathered from telescope observation

   c. finding cures for diseases

   d. writing observations

   e. collecting information

   f. studying climate

1. Which phrase(s) fit into the category of a scientist's job? _____

_____

_____

_____

2. Which phrase(s) fit into the category of ways that meteorologists (scientists who study the weather) make predictions? _____

_____

_____

_____

3. Which phrase(s) fit into the category of an animal behaviorist's job? _____

_____

_____

_____

4. Name a category in which all of these phrases fit. _____

_____

_____

_____

Exercise II

Directions: Organize the following words into as many categories as possible. List the categories and the words grouped within them in the spaces provided. You must list at least three words in each category that you create. You may use the same word in more than one category.

Try to create categories that no one else will!

star	see	lobster	crow	man	walnut
treasure	creator	wave	stove	woman	October
July	fox	mountain	pocket	crazy	September
drummer	potato	cashew	strawberry	highway	volcano
earthquake	ax	hammer	dog	queen	meteor
goat	stew	sloppy	sponge	August	rat
Octopus	river	ostrich	crater	square	June
saw	stone	fish	earth	ribbon	drill
valley	shark	November	onion	canary	hill
rake	whale				

CATEGORY _____

Words _____

_____

_____

_____

CATEGORY _____

Words _____

_____

_____

_____

CATEGORY _____

Words _____

_____

_____

_____

CATEGORY _____

Words _____

_____

_____

_____

CATEGORY _____

Words _____

_____

_____

_____

CATEGORY _____

Words _____

_____

_____

_____

CATEGORY _____

Words _____

_____

_____

_____

CATEGORY _____

Words _____

_____

_____

_____

CATEGORY _____

Words _____

_____

_____

_____

CATEGORY _____

Words _____

_____

_____

_____

CATEGORY _____

Words _____

_____

_____

_____

CATEGORY _____

Words _____

_____

_____

_____

Unit V Summary

A category is a name for a group of ideas or pieces of information that have something in common. For example, city, state, town, and village all fit into the category of units of government. When you organize ideas and information into categories, you can usually remember them better. Also you will discover how ideas and information are similar and how they are different.

Technology Adaptation

- Choose artifact items from diverse categories such as: shells, coins, minerals, and so on. Organize the items by category. Search for pictures or articles of these items online and create a presentation to virtually display these items (and their categories) to the class.

- Take an inventory of items in the classroom. Develop categories and, using a computer, create a form using an application like Google Docs. In the form, record categories and lists. Then partner with another student and share the form. Identify similarities and differences in the categories based on your lists. Share the results in a presentation to the class.

- Use a class blog to explain why what you learned in the lesson is important.

UNIT VI
PICTURING IN YOUR MIND'S EYE

Introduction

It is sometimes important to imagine what something looks like. It may be when reading fiction or it may be when reading a history or science book. The key to understanding what is being read may be in your ability to imagine it.

This unit will help you practice using your imagination.

Exercise I

Directions: Your teacher will read a selection aloud called "The Body's Defense Against Disease." As you listen, try to picture the following things:

1. The first line of defense is described as an obstacle course. Try to picture the obstacles that get in the way of germs.

2. Part of the second line of defense is the white blood cells. Try to picture what the white blood cells look like as they surround a germ.

3. The third line of defense is antibodies. When you hear about antibodies, try to form a picture of them.

4. As you hear about the following things, try to get a picture of each one in your mind's eye: germs, lymph, capillaries, and infection.

When the reading is completed, you will be asked to answer some factual questions.

Again, it might help you to close your eyes so you can picture things without interference as you listen.

Answer These Questions

    1. Name three things that provide an obstacle course in the body's first line of defense.

_____

_____

_____

    2. How do white blood cells help the body protect you from germs?

_____

_____

_____

    3. What is a capillary?

_____

_____

_____

    4. What does an antibody do to protect you from germs?

_____

_____

_____

    5. How does lymph help your body to handle germs?

_____

_____

_____

For Fun

    1. Draw a germ as you pictured it.

2. Did any other interesting visual images come into your mind as you listened? If so, draw or explain them in words.

Kinds of Pictures in Your Mind's Eye

When people imagine, they often see pictures or images in their mind's eye. Sometimes the imagination includes other senses as well: hearing, smelling, touching, even tasting. In fact, when some people imagine, they don't see pictures at all. Instead they hear, smell, touch, taste, or all of these.

Everyone can imagine, but we all use our imagination in our own personal way. What do you experience when *you* imagine? Write your answer on the lines provided.

_____

_____

_____

_____

_____

_____

_____

_____

Solve Your Problems by Picturing the Steps

Sometimes you have an idea for a project you want to do. You can picture, or see in your mind's eye, a completed task. For example, you can imagine the tent when it is set up. You can imagine how to successfully play a video game. You can imagine how you might build a fort with plastic blocks.

However, when you start to work on the project, you find that the picture in your mind isn't as helpful as you had hoped. You don't know how to begin.

Exercise II

Directions: Following you will find three methods for making a paper airplane. Try to use each method, and discover which one works best for you. Use imagery to picture each step as you go.

Method I

Study the picture. Then take one of the sheets that your teacher gave you. Try to construct the paper airplane pictured.

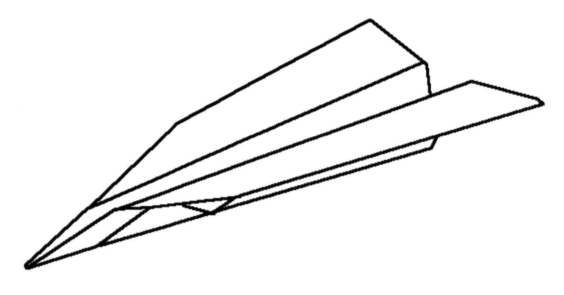

Method II

Read the step-by-step instructions that follow. Follow each of the steps. Try to construct the paper airplane they describe.

Step 1

Use a sheet of 8½ × 11" paper. Crease-fold the paper in half first. Then open it. Fold the top corners down.

Step 2

Hold the paper lengthwise. Call the top left point A and the bottom left point B. Fold A and B down about a quarter of the sides to the crease. Make sure A and B touch on the center crease.

Step 3

Call the top points of the airplane's nose C and D. Fold in points C and D. The top two edges should meet each other on the center crease.

Step 4

Fold the entire airplane in half in the opposite direction.

Step 5

Fold the wings down to meet the bottom edge of the fuselage.

Step 6

Curl the tail section up slightly for better lift.

Method III

Look at the pictures in the steps below. The pictures show what the airplane should look like *as* you follow the directions for each step. Try to match what you are doing to what you see.

Step 1

Use a sheet of 8½ × 11" paper. Crease-fold the paper in half first. Then open it. Fold the top corners down.

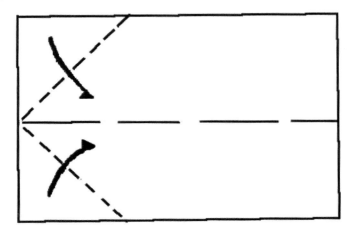

Step 2

Fold in the sides. Make sure that points A and B touch each other on the center crease.

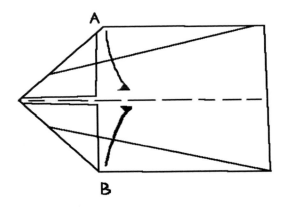

Step 3

Fold in points C and D. The top two edges should meet each other on the center crease.

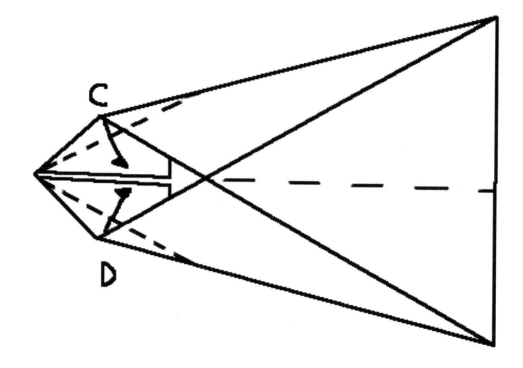

Step 4

Fold the entire airplane in half in the opposite direction.

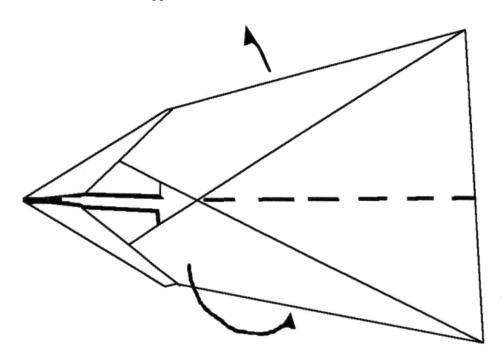

Step 5

Fold the wings down to meet the bottom edge of the fuselage.

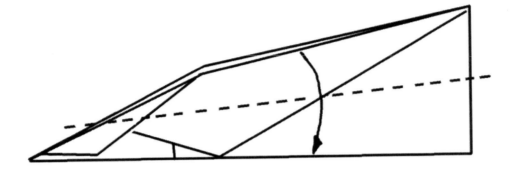

Step 6

Curl the tail section up slightly for better lift.

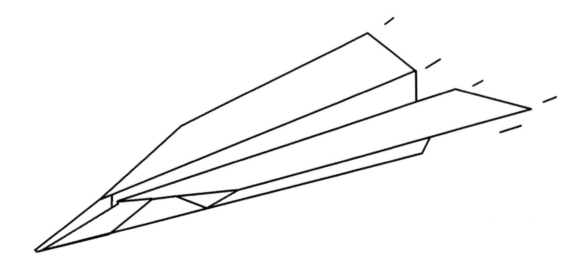

Directions: Fill in the graphic organizer with the following vocabulary words.

Word	Definition	Picture of Word
Antonym		
Base Word		
Capitalization		
Comma		
Conjunction		
Context Clues		
Editing		
Exposition		
Fact		
Fiction		
Interjection		

Unit VI Summary

Most people have the ability to imagine or see pictures in their mind's eye. Sometimes the imagination uses your other senses: hearing, smelling, feeling, and even tasting.

These pictures or images can help to make reading and hearing stories more interesting to you. You can also remember important details when you form images of them.

The ability to picture things in your mind's eye is often helpful in solving problems. When you use your imagination to help you solve a problem, break the problem down into small, easy-to-do steps. Then do one step at a time.

Technology Adaptation

- Draw pictures of vocabulary words using the computer program Paint (for Windows) or Paintbrush (for Mac).

IMPROVING YOUR MEMORY

A Memory Game

Directions: In this game, you'll find six different groups of letters. They are lined up in different ways to make it easier for you to concentrate on one group at a time.

Read over group 1 below. Then cover it with your hand. How many of the letters can you remember? Write all the letters from group 1 that you can remember on the line below that group. Repeat for groups 2–6.

6. g t j
   x k r d
   n a q l
   i c

1. d h r c w j v

_____   _____

3. f m z u g w k s a p n r l   _____

_____   _____

                                          _____

2. r l s
   v q i
   x a g

5. a b c d l m n o v w x y z

_____

_____

_____

_____   4. t k q d y a f

_____

Learning about Your Memory

There are two levels of memory: short-term memory and long-term memory.

Short-term memory is what you can keep in your attention in the moment. Most people can remember only five to nine different things in their short-term memories. That is why you can remember 7 letters easily and 9 letters with a little more difficulty. Yet most people cannot remember 10 letters or more.

Long-term memory is what you know and can bring to mind whenever you choose to do so. What is in your long-term memory stays with you for a long time. If you review it now and then, you can remember it as long as you like.

You could probably remember the 13 letters in group 5 because this group contains three sequences of letters that are already part of your long-term memory: a, b, c, d, l, m, n, o, v, w, x, y, z. To remember this group, you really needed only to remember the first letter in each sequence and the length of the sequence.

Another Memory Game

Directions: Read list A twice. Then cover the list with your hand, and write down in the blanks as many words from list A as you can recall. Next, turn the book so you can read list B. Do the same with list B as you did with list A.

List A

pharmacy	heat
spruce	bakery
gas	elm
oak	friction
office	theater
density	maple
fir	hotel
restaurant	

_____

_____

_____

_____

_____

How many words did you correctly recall?

_____

List B

Birds	Places to Play Sports	Scientific Terms
robin	gym	orbit
sparrow	park	force
hawk	rink	conservation
eagle	pool	phase
crow	field	element

_____
_____
_____
_____
_____

How many words did you correctly recall?

_____

Ways to Remember

This unit will show you four different ways to remember: grouping, visualizing, repeating, and choosing to remember. Each of these ways can help you to "move" information *from short-term memory into long-term memory*.

Ways to Remember: Grouping

In "Another Memory Game," you were probably able to remember more of the words in list B than in list A. The words in list A were not in any order. The words in list B were organized into three groups.

When information is grouped, it is easier to remember. Grouping means to organize information so that details are brought together under the main idea or category that connects them. For example, in "Another Memory Game," each column in list B includes five words that are examples of the category listed in the heading.

Grouping information is one way of helping to "move" it from short-term to long-term memory. When you want to remember ideas and information, try to organize them into groups that make sense to you. For example, put details with main ideas that they support. List examples with categories that they illustrate. When you group ideas and facts together, remembering one will help you to recall the others.

Exercise I

Directions: Think about information that you need to learn and remember for this class that can be grouped in some way.

Write the names of two groups of such information on the top line in the space provided. Then list at least four details or examples for each group.

Group #1:	Group #2:

Ways to Remember: Visualizing

Visualizing means to see an image or picture in your mind's eye. For example, close your eyes right now, and visualize a mental picture of the room where you are sitting. Try this just for a few seconds. When you see this mental picture, you are visualizing.

Practice visualizing again. Close your eyes, and see the face of a friend of yours. Notice how clearly you can see the details of her or his face.

One way to use visualizing is to see a mental picture for each main idea that you want to remember. When you want to remember something, visualize a picture of it in your mind. For many people, a mental picture is easier to remember than words are. See as clear an image as you can, and examine it for a few seconds. Then let it disappear.

Some people don't visualize clearly. If you don't, you can learn to visualize more clearly by practicing. Look at an object or a picture with your eyes. Then close your eyes and try to visualize it. The more you practice, the clearer your mental pictures will become.

Draw a picture in the space provided of something you visualized in your mind.

Did the picture you drew of what you visualized help you remember better? Why or why not?

_____

_____

_____

_____

Ways to Remember: Repeating

Another good way to remember is to repeat information you want to learn. Be sure to say it in your own words. Even though you have already learned something, go over it one more time. When you repeat information in this way, it will help you move it into your long-term memory and will keep the information available to you.

One good way to repeat information is to say it aloud to yourself. When you say it aloud, not only do you speak the information, but you also hear it.

Ways to Remember: Choosing to Remember

You can always remember more effectively when you choose to remember. The more you want to learn and know, the more you will be able to remember what you have learned.

To choose to remember, you need to pay attention to and be interested in what you are learning.

Mnemonics

Mnemonic methods are ways of remembering more efficiently. Two mnemonic methods are acronyms and acrostics.

Acronyms

An acronym is a word that is made by taking the first letter from each word that you want to remember and making a new word from all of those letters.

Exercise II

Directions: Try to create acronyms for remembering the two groups of information that follows. Write each acronym on the line below the information that it represents.

1. The Great Lakes: Superior, Huron, Michigan, Erie, Ontario.

   Hint: you can put the names of the lakes in any helpful order.

   _____

2. The colors of visible light in the spectrum and the order in which they appear: red, orange, yellow, green, blue, indigo, violet.

   Hint: an acronym can be more than one word.

   _____

Exercise III

Directions: Can you create any acronyms that can help you remember information that you need to know? List any acronyms that you can create in the space provided.

_____

_____

_____

_____

_____

Acrostics

An acrostic is a sentence that is made by taking the first letter from each word or symbol that you want to remember and then inserting another word beginning with the same letter. For example, to help you remember the lines on a musical staff, the acrostic is: <u>E</u>very <u>G</u>ood <u>B</u>oy <u>D</u>oes <u>F</u>ine.

Good Boys Do Fine Always
All Cows Eat Grass

Every Good Boy Does Fine
FACE

E—Every

G—Good

B—Boy

D—Does

F—Fine

Another useful acrostic can help you remember the classification system of living things in biology: King Phillip came over for green stamps.

Kingdom—K—King

Phylum—P—Phillip

Class—C—came

Order—O—over

Family—F—for

Genus—G—green

Species—S—stamps

Do you know any acrostics that have been useful to you?

_____

_____

_____

Other Mnemonic Methods

There are many other mnemonic methods, and they include methods for remembering names and numbers, errands and appointments, and other kinds of information.

If you want to learn more about mnemonic methods, there are many exercises found online and many books in the school or public library. All you need to do is practice!

Unit VII Summary

- There are two levels of memory: short-term memory and long-term memory.

- Short-term memory is what you can keep in your attention in the moment. Most people can only remember five to nine different things in their short-term memories.

- Long-term memory is what you know and can bring to mind whenever you choose to do so.

- An important part of learning is "moving" information from your short-term memory into your long-term memory. Four ways to accomplish this are:

  o Grouping information: To group information is to organize it so that details are brought together under the main idea or category that connects them.

  o Visualizing information: To visualize information is to see an image or picture of it in your mind's eye.

  o Repeating information: To repeat information is to put the information in your own words and go over it. Say it aloud to yourself so you can hear it as well as speak it.

  o Choosing to remember: The more you choose to remember, the more you will remember. To choose to remember, you need to want to pay attention to and be interested in what you are learning.

- Mnemonics is the art of remembering. Mnemonic methods are ways of remembering more efficiently. Two useful mnemonics methods are:

  o Acronym: An acronym is a word that is made by taking the first letter from each word you want to remember and making a new word from all of those letters.

  o Acrostic: An acrostic is a sentence that is made by taking the first letter from each word or symbol you want to remember and inserting another word beginning with that same letter.

Technology Adaptation

- Search online for memory exercises or memory games. Prepare a multimedia presentation to demonstrate to others how to use the method you discovered.

- Produce a diagram using mapping notes. You can also use free websites to list your ideas and create the diagram automatically. Some examples include:

  o spidescribe.net—allows users to easily visualize their ideas by connecting various pieces of information together. The site also combines elements like text, images, and other files.

  o editstorm—allows users to work on ideas and organize them into sticky notes for others to see.

  o bubbl.us—great site for mind-mapping and brainstorming. It allows users to create concept maps easily and with minimal tools. You can invite others to join in as editors to your mind map.

UNIT VIII
ORGANIZING IDEAS

Introduction

The unit "Putting Ideas Together" presented how organizing ideas and information into categories can improve memory. This skill is useful in many other ways. For example, you can find clothes in a drawer more easily if each drawer holds a certain category or type of clothes. You can find information in a school notebook more efficiently if there are categories or sections. You would even find cooking an easier task if like ingredients are stored in categories or on certain shelves in the kitchen.

When you organize ideas and information into categories, the name of each category you create is a main idea. Each idea or piece of information in the category is a detail. In the shopping list below, the main ideas are at the top of each list of details.

Example Situation

You have to go shopping, and you only have a certain amount of time. You have to find the things on your list quickly. So you organize your list into the sections of the grocery store:

Dairy	Baking Goods	Produce	Frozen Foods
milk	baking soda	oranges	ice cream
eggs	chocolate chips	celery	microwavable dinner
yogurt	yeast	lettuce	frozen corn
butter	brown sugar	carrots	
cheese	flour	radishes	
	baking powder	spinach	
		apples	

Exercise I

Directions: Read the following situations. Each situation requires you to make a list so that you can do the work more efficiently.

Make a list that has main ideas for headings. Place the details below the correct main ideas. Your lists should look something like the shopping list on the "Example Situation." Please feel free to shorten the details into notes.

Situation A

You have a test for science class tomorrow on animal characteristics. You are required to know the characteristics of amphibians, mammals, and birds.

You must know which of the characteristics below fits with what kind of animal:

- feeds young with mammary glands

- lives in water and on land

- has wings

- reproduces by laying eggs

- reproduces by giving birth to young animal

- has hair

- has gill-breathing larvae

- has hollow bones

- has backbones

- has feathers

- has gelatinous eggs

First write your main ideas. Then organize the list of details in the spaces below. You may use a detail more than once.

Main Ideas: _____   _____   _____

Details: _____   _____   _____

_____   _____   _____

_____   _____   _____

_____   _____   _____

_____   _____   _____

Situation B

You have to write a biography about a famous person. You have to answer these questions about the person:

1. What happened in the person's early years?

2. What kind of education did the person receive?

3. What made this person famous?

You choose Abraham Lincoln because you already know the following about him: he walked three miles to school each way to get a good education; his mother was Nancy Hanks; he had one sister; his father was Thomas Lincoln; the family moved from Kentucky to Indiana when Lincoln was young; he went to school to become a lawyer; he could write well; he debated Stephen Douglass; he was a captain in the Black Hawk War; he trained as a store clerk; and he became sixteenth president of the United States.

First write your main ideas. Then organize your list. Add any other details that you know.

Main Ideas: _____   _____   _____

Details: _____   _____   _____

_____   _____   _____

_____   _____   _____

_____   _____   _____

_____   _____   _____

Exercise II

Directions: Read situation A and follow the directions at the end of the situation. Do the same for situation B.

Situation A

Before you can get this week's allowance, your parents insist that you do the following chores:

make bed each day

study for math test

put away clean clothes

mow the lawn

pick up dirty clothes

work on social studies report

load the dishwasher

feed and water the pets

read three chapters in the novel for English class

In the space provided, make lists of all the chores you have to do. Make sure each list has an appropriate main idea for a heading.

Main Ideas: _____ _____ _____

Details: _____ _____ _____

_____ _____ _____

_____ _____ _____

_____ _____ _____

_____ _____ _____

Situation B

You are going on an overnight camping trip with family friends. It is your assignment to bring the following items: sleeping bag, bottled water, lantern, board game, playing cards, fruit, cereal, doughnuts, life jacket, flashlight, extra blankets, fishing gear, peanut butter and crackers, and a tarp.

In the space provided, categorize the items you are assigned to bring. Make sure each list has an appropriate main idea for a heading. Create your list in the space provided.

Main Ideas: _____ _____ _____

Details: _____ _____ _____

_____ _____ _____

_____ _____ _____

_____ _____ _____

Topics

A topic is broader or larger than a main idea. It can include several main ideas.

Exercise III

Directions: Read statements 1 through 4 below, and answer the questions on the lines provided.

1. The topic of situation A in Exercise I might be living things or animals. Is there any other topic these ideas might fit under?

   _____

2. The topic of situation B in Exercise I might be presidents or famous politicians. Can you think of any other topic it could be?

   _____

3. The topic of situation A in Exercise II might be chores or ways to earn money. Can you think of another topic that would fit these ideas?

   _____

4. The topic of situation B in Exercise II might be Scout trips or hiking plans. Can you think of another topic that would fit these ideas?

   _____

Exercise IV

Directions: Read the lists in #1 below. Create a topic for the main ideas and details in #1, and write it on the line provided. Do the same for #2.

1.

Food	Favors	Activities	To Do
cake	napkins	video game	get a cake
ice cream	noisemakers	outdoor sports	send invites
snacks	hats	board game	go shopping
hamburgers	prizes	contests	set up for party

rolls   bake brownies

ketchup/mustard

brownies

The topic is_____

2.

Early Years	Education	Events Leading to Fame
one of seven	taught by older brother	became leader of Virginia militia
father died when young	no formal schooling	member of the First Continental Congress
favored son	learned surveying	General of the Continental Army
raised in Virginia	took over brother's military duties	commander at Valley Forge
took over Mount Vernon at a young age	surveyed wilderness of America	first president of the United States

The topic is_____

Exercise V

Directions: Pick a topic from the suggestions listed. Circle the topic. Then in the spaces provided, write out three lists showing main ideas and details that fit with this topic.

World War II	mammals	famous authors
famous women	automobiles	famous politicians
vacation spots	schools	flight
television	technology	agriculture
pets	entertainment	food
clothing	careers	twentieth century
plant kingdom	books	explorers

Main Ideas: _____   _____   _____

Details: _____   _____   _____

_____   _____   _____

_____   _____   _____

_____   _____   _____

_____   _____   _____

Unit VIII Summary

A category name is also a main idea. The ideas and information within a category are the details of that main idea.

Details give more information about or support about a main idea.

A topic is broader or larger than a main idea. It often includes several main ideas.

DETAILS are part of MAIN IDEAS are part of a TOPIC

or

A TOPIC includes MAIN IDEAS are supported by DETAILS

Technology Adaptation

- Create a website with other classmates or work individually to create a website. There are free website resources such as Weebly.com to create a simple website for free.

- The terms *topic*, *main idea*, and *supporting details* discussed in this unit are found in virtually every website. The "topic" of a website is usually the broad intent of what the website will offer potential users. The "main ideas" are then major subcategories based on the overall topic, while the "supporting details" are simply data. An example would be for you and your classmates to create a website for organizing a talent show in your school. "Talent show" would be the topic, and main ideas might include: community event, fund-raiser, building school culture and tradition, and having fun. Supporting details (or data) would be where and when the show will be held, how auditions are conducted, what prizes are awarded, how much tickets will cost, and so on. Present your website to the class. If the topic of the website is school related (such as the talent show example) consider asking school officials if the project could be conducted.

- Create a website for: keeping statistics about the local weather, creating a book list and allowing for blogs or reviews for those books online, and planning a community service event.

- Create a form using an application like Google Docs. In the form, create your own topic and suggested lists like you completed in the exercises in this unit. Then share the form with other classmates and see if others can provide the main ideas and supporting details for your topic.

- Create a PowerPoint or Prezi to present a class report by selecting a topic that interests you and presenting main ideas and supporting details on the topic. This is a "show and tell"–type exercise using technology.

READING FOR MEANING

How Do You Read?

"Read the assignment in your book, and be ready for a quiz!"

This is a direction you probably often hear in school. When you are given this direction, what do you do?

Look at the reading "The Race to the Moon" in this unit. If your teacher asked you to read this and be ready for a quiz about it, what would you do? On the lines below, briefly describe *how* you would complete this assignment.

Remember: Don't actually read the section now. Just describe each step you would use and *how* you would read it.

_____

_____

_____

_____

_____

The Race to the Moon

Sputnik Launched!

On October 4, 1957, the U.S.S.R. astounded the American public by launching Sputnik I. Sputnik I was the first man-made satellite to orbit the earth. On November 3rd of the same year, the Soviets sent another Sputnik, Sputnik II, into orbit, carrying a dog named Laika. The race to the moon was on.

The United States Responds

The United States was caught off guard by the advanced technology of the Soviet space program. In the year following the launching of Sputnik I, the U.S. Congress authorized billions of dollars to be put into an American space program. NASA, the National Aeronautics and Space Administration, was created in 1958. In that same year the United States launched its first satellite, Explorer I.

The First Travelers in Space

A few years later the Soviet Union sent the first traveler into outer space. On April 7, 1961, Yuri Gagarin became the first man to journey into the farthest reaches of the Earth's atmosphere. In 1963 Valentina Tereshkova became the first woman to fly into outer space.

The First American Astronaut

In the years between 1961 and 1963 the American space program was also busy. The United States launched its first manned flight in May 1961. Alan Shepherd rode a tiny capsule that was launched from Cape Canaveral in Florida. Shepherd's flight lasted only fifteen minutes. Americans huddled around their TV sets to watch the launch. Telstar, the first communications satellite, was also launched in 1961.

Amazing Breakthroughs in 1965

Amazing breakthroughs engineered by both countries took place in 1965. Leonov of the U.S.S.R. made the first space walk from the Voshkod spacecraft. The United States launched the first of the Gemini space flights, each of which orbited the Earth many times. Luna 9 of the U.S.S.R. and Surveyor I of the United States were both unmanned spacecraft that made soft landings on the moon during this year. A Soviet probe crash-landed on Venus. And the United States' Mariner 4 transmitted the first close-up pictures of Mars over a distance of 217 million kilometers.

Orbiting the Moon

After many different kinds of space experiments had been conducted by both nations, the United States made a great thrust to the moon in 1968. The American astronauts Frank Borman, William Anders, and James Lovell Jr. orbited the moon ten times on December 24–25 of that year.

Moon Landing!

Finally in July 1969 American astronauts Armstrong and Aldrin placed their feet on the surface of the moon. The race between nations was over. The plaque the astronauts left on the moon said: "Here men from Earth first set forth on the moon. July 1969 A.D. We came in peace for all mankind."

Introduction

Many students don't have a special way of reading a textbook. They may start with the first word in the assignment and read as far as they get. Unfortunately, this isn't a very good way to learn from reading.

This unit will show you a way of reading an assignment in a textbook and learning from what was read. This method is called *reading for meaning*. You may find that this method is new to you and will take a little more time at first. You might also find it a little tricky. Stay with it! Learn how to use this method, and you will become a better learner.

Remember, the goal for reading is not to just finish; the goal is to *understand* after you have finished the text.

Reading for Meaning

When you read a paragraph or section in your textbook, what you really want to find out is:

What is the *main idea* of this reading?

What are the *important details* that support the *main idea?*

Reading for meaning means locating *main ideas* and the *supporting details* in your reading.

Another way to think of *reading for meaning* is this: when you read for meaning, you're trying to find out what the paragraph or section is trying to tell you. Ask yourself these questions:

What does the person who wrote this paragraph or section want me to know?

What is this paragraph or section trying to tell me?

Exercise I

Directions: Read the paragraph below. Then write the main idea of the paragraph on the lines that follow.

Remember: The *main idea* in a paragraph is the most important idea. The *main idea* is the idea that the writer is trying to share with you.

Paragraph A

Dogs have a very powerful sense of smell that they can use to find things. Police use tracking dogs to search for people who are missing in the woods. The dogs sniff a piece of clothing owned by the missing person. Then they try to track the scent in the area where the person was last seen. Often these dogs can find people who are lost when the police have no other way of locating them. Another kind of tracking dog is the hunting hound. These dogs can follow animals for miles through the forest once they have sniffed their scent. Though some dogs are better than others in using their sense of smell, all dogs have a stronger sense of smell than people do.

Main idea: _____

_____

_____

_____

_____

Main Idea and Supporting Details

We know that the *main idea* of a paragraph is the most important idea in that paragraph.

Most paragraphs also have *supporting details*. Supporting details explain, prove, or tell something about the main idea of the paragraph. They make the main idea more clear to us or give us more information about it.

These details are called *supporting* details because they "hold up" the main idea. This means that they give us reasons to believe the main idea and help us to understand it.

Exercise II

Directions: Read paragraph A again. On the lines below, list *three* supporting details for the main idea.

1. _____

2. _____

3. _____

Exercise III

Directions: Find the main idea for the paragraph that follows. Then locate two supporting details. Write the main idea and supporting details on the appropriate lines. Do the same for paragraphs C and D.

Paragraph B

In the early days America was a country full of individuals who did many things well. One man stands out from all the rest. This man helped to organize many institutions in the new country: the U.S. Post Office; the Pennsylvania Academy; Pennsylvania Hospital, the first in America. He also organized the first American expedition to the Arctic region. He was an inventor, inventing many useful things including the Franklin stove, the lightning rod, bifocal glasses, and an instrument he called the "Armonica." He also wrote books and newspapers and took part in the politics of early America. Benjamin Franklin was a man of many talents.

Main idea: _____

_____

_____

Supporting details:

1. _____

2. _____

Paragraph C

She was an adult female who died three million years ago. The archaeologists who found her bones nicknamed her "Lucy." They did not find her entire skeleton. However, a description of Lucy can be based on the bones they found. She was a Hominidae, a primate that stood and walked on two legs. She had a skeleton much like ours. But she was tiny compared to today's humans. She stood three feet, eight inches tall and weighed about 65 pounds. Her thick bones show that she must have had great muscular strength. Lucy's face and apelike jutting jaws were large, but her brain was probably only one-third the size of a modern human's.

Main idea: _____

_____

_____

Supporting details:

1. _____

2. _____

Paragraph D

The man lowered a hydrophone into the water. This phone was meant to pick up the clicks, whistles, and short piercing screams of the killer whales. He explained that the clicks seem to be a way that the whales tell each other where food is located. The whistles are heard most often between resting or socializing whales. But, he explained, the most interesting of all are the screams. They are different within each whale pod (a pod is a group of whales). This suggests that whales are among the few animals that have a local dialect or a special way of speaking to the others that live in the same region.

Main idea: _____

_____

_____

Supporting details:

1. _____

2. _____

How Do You Find the Main Idea?

The main idea of a paragraph is stated in the *topic sentence*. The purpose of the *topic sentence* is to tell you the main idea. For example, in the paragraph about the strong sense of smell that dogs have, the topic sentence is the first one.

When you read a paragraph, the main idea will sometimes be very clear to you. When it's not clear, use these hints for finding it:

1. Most often the topic sentence is the first sentence in the paragraph. This means that you'll often find the main idea in the first sentence of a paragraph.

2. Sometimes the topic sentence is the last sentence in a paragraph. When the first sentence doesn't tell you the main idea, look at the last sentence in the paragraph and see if it's there.

3. In some paragraphs, the topic sentence is in the middle of the paragraph. In these paragraphs, you can only find the main idea by reading the paragraph carefully and figuring out what the paragraph is telling you.

4. In some paragraphs, there is no topic sentence. The main idea is not stated clearly in any one sentence of the paragraph. Often this happens when the main idea has already been stated in another paragraph. When this happens, you really have to read carefully to see if you can figure out what the paragraph is trying to tell you.

How to Read for Meaning

Reading for meaning means finding the main idea and supporting details in your reading. You can read for meaning by using these four steps:

- surveying

- reading

- mapping

- checking yourself

Step 1: Surveying

When you first start to read a paragraph, don't read it word for word. Instead *survey* the paragraph first.

Surveying means to look quickly at any heading or titles over the paragraph and then read the first and last sentences. *Surveying* will usually let you find out what the paragraph's main idea is. And it takes only a minute or less!

Exercise IV

Directions: *Survey* the paragraph that follows. On the lines below it, write what you think the *main idea* of this paragraph is.

A Profit in Frogs

People don't usually think of frog raising as a profitable business, but many people are willing to pay for frogs. Universities and high schools buy frogs for use in their science labs. Restaurants will pay $4.50 or more for a pound of dressed frog meat, as frogs are considered a delicacy by many people. NASA uses frogs in space and will pay $25 or more for a healthy bullfrog. Probably more frogs have orbited the earth than people. People who own ponds will also buy frogs because frogs can help to keep down the insect population. So, the next time you think about leaving a frog in your teacher's desk, you may decide that there's a more profitable use for your hopping, green friend.

_____

_____

_____

_____

_____

Step 2: Reading

Once you've *surveyed* a paragraph, you usually have a sense of what the *main idea* is. Now *read* the paragraph at your normal rate of reading. As you *read*, look for *supporting details* that prove, explain, or tell you more about the main idea.

Exercise V

Directions: Read the paragraph about "A Profit in Frogs." As you read, be sure to look for supporting details. List at least two details on the lines below.

_____

_____

Step 3: Mapping

Mapping is a way of taking notes about your reading. Look at the *map* below for the paragraph about frogs.

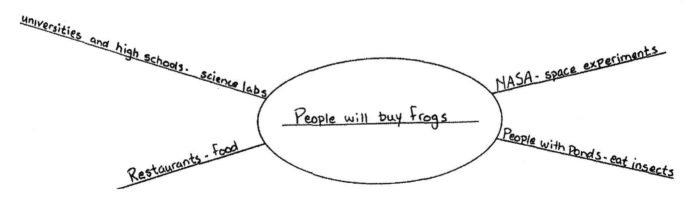

You can take *mapping* notes in this way:

1. First, write the *main idea* on a line in the middle of your paper. Then circle the *main idea*.

2. Write each *supporting detail* you find on a line that touches the circle around the *main idea*.

Mapping is a way of taking notes that helps you to understand what the main idea is and what the supporting details are.

Exercise VI

Directions: Survey the paragraph below. Then read it and take notes in the *map* below the paragraph.

Smart Chimps!

Chimpanzees are among the most intelligent animals on earth other than human beings. The structure or makeup of the chimpanzee brain is a lot like the structure of the human brain. Chimps have the ability to use simple tools. In recent years, scientists have found that chimps communicate with each other through noises and gestures. Chimps also seem to be able to learn words and make signs that stand for words.

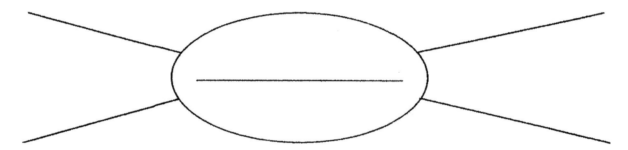

Step 4: Checking Yourself

Now, look at your mapping notes and *check yourself*. Using only your notes, tell yourself what you learned. Or tell someone who hasn't read the paragraph.

When you take a little time to *check yourself*, you'll see what you have learned. And you'll find it much easier to remember what you have read.

Exercise VII

Directions: Go back and look through the four steps. They are surveying, reading, mapping, and checking yourself.

Then use the four steps to *read for meaning* the following three paragraphs.

Visitors from Outer Space

You may not believe in extraterrestrial life forms, but the fact is that we get "visitors" from outer space daily. Each year at least 20,000 tons of material from meteors enters our atmosphere. This means about 50 tons a day! Chances of the meteors being big enough to cause us any harm are incredibly slim. The earth's atmosphere burns up the material from outer space before it can reach the surface of the earth. Only 10 to 20 new meteors are actually found on the earth's surface each year. But as they enter the earth's atmosphere, the burning can be seen from earth as a streak of light. So, we should be able to locate a "falling star" on any clear night.

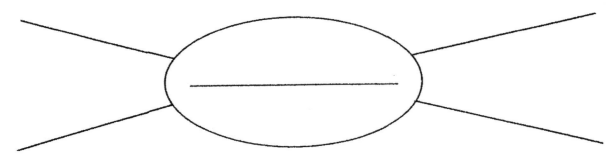

The World Has Been Round for a Long Time!

Some say that Columbus discovered that the world was round. This is not entirely true. Many people knew the world was round long before the days of Columbus. The Greek mathematician Pythagoras declared that the world was round in the sixth century B.C. A few hundred years later, the Greek scholar Eratosthenes figured the distance around the world. During the same time period, Aristotle reported rumors of lands on the other side of the globe. The Greek mapmaker Strabo wrote of men's attempts to sail around the world in the seventh century A.D. Many well-educated men of Columbus's day agreed with Columbus that it was perfectly possible to reach the east by sailing west because the earth was a sphere. So, you see, the idea that the earth is round has been around for a long time.

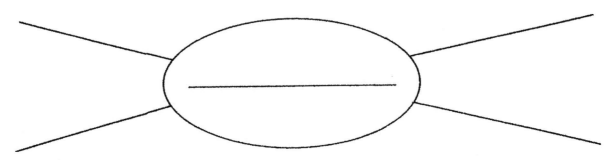

The Gentle Ape

It's hard to imagine any relative of King Kong as being gentle. But according to Dr. Francine Paterson, the 230-pound Koko is just that. Koko is a lowland female gorilla who has been working with Dr. Paterson for over a decade. By the use of sign language, Koko let Dr. Paterson know that she wanted a kitten for her birthday. When Paterson gave her a little kitten, Koko was delighted. She spent many hours playing with the tiny animal, carrying her kitten from place to place, gently stroking its fur, and bending over to give it a kiss. When the kitten died, Koko was struck with deep grief. It wasn't until the kitten was replaced that Koko resumed her normal activities. It might also interest you to know that Koko is a vegetarian. She obviously prefers petting small creatures to eating them!

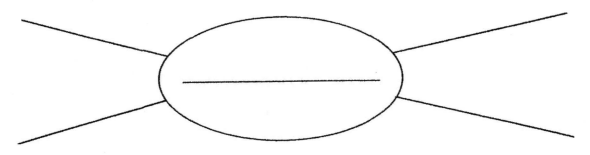

Unit IX Summary

Reading for meaning means locating *main ideas* and the important *supporting details* in your reading.

The *main idea* in a paragraph is the most important idea. It is the idea that the rest of the paragraph is about.

Supporting details explain, prove, or tell something more about the main idea. They make the main idea more clear or give more information about it.

The main idea of a paragraph is often stated in the *topic sentence*. Most often the topic sentence is the first sentence in the paragraph. It can also be the last sentence or in the middle of the paragraph.

How do you *read for meaning*? Use these four steps:

1. Surveying: Look quickly at any headings or titles above the paragraph. Then read the first and last sentences of the paragraph. Surveying will usually help you find out what the *main idea* is.

2. Reading: Read the paragraph at your normal rate of reading. As you read, look for *supporting details.*

3. Mapping: Make a map like the one that follows to take notes from your reading. Mapping helps you to learn the *main idea* and *supporting details* of the reading. It also gives you a record of the reading that you can use later.

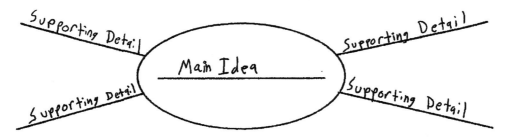

4. Checking yourself: Look at your mapping notes and tell yourself what the reading is about. Or ask yourself: What have I learned from reading this?

Technology Adaptation

- Work with a partner to create a Google Doc. Skim back over the unit and list the most useful information.

- Find an article online that is interesting and engaging to you. Practice skimming it to find the main idea. Next, make a list of the supporting details. Explain what was read to a classmate who is unfamiliar with the topic.

- Make an electronic graphic organizer. Read a section of the text and complete the organizer electronically.

UNIT X
READING ONLINE AND USING ONLINE TEXTS

Introduction

In our fast-paced world, the Internet delivers quick and easy access to information. The art of actually reading digital text may seem appealing, but the value of using a book for seeking information and learning still has a valid place for students. Reading and using texts from traditional print mediums versus online formats presents many different challenges for learners. Although technology and the Internet has made many electronic books, research databases, journals, blogs, and other sources widely available through electronic retrieval, deciphering what is useful and even reliable information can be difficult. Further, actually reading online poses its own set of challenges.

Reading from digital text requires a degree of self-control to remain focused on the topic and not distracted by other applications or web pages. Most basic-level researchers perform a simple surface-level search of the Internet, read the information retrieved (for pleasure or for research), and then consider that information "good enough" and move on. While this may be suitable, it often does not provide the depth and breadth required for quality learning. In these exercises, you will be given an opportunity to understand what is available online, how to properly search, how to determine what is and what is not a good web source, and finally how to "weed out" bad information.

Exercise I

Directions: Complete one or more of the following to integrate reading and using online texts.

1. Perform a search for the state of Hawaii. Suggested search engines are Google.com, Bing.com, Yahoo.com, and Ask.com. Search engines usually return ten or so websites per page. Using these results, review three to five of the returned choices. Look for one source that looks like an encyclopedia article on the topic.

2. Determine if the entry is user edited, or if it is from a valid source such as a commercial company like World Book.

3. Next, review a choice that is in the form of a blog or forum where users have commented on the published content.

4. Next, look for a visual source such as YouTube.

5. Finally, look for a web page that displays an entry that was published by a university or other "expert voice." This kind of web page may be a study that was conducted to prove or disprove a hypothesis, for example.

6. Compare what you have found by creating a T-chart. Do this by drawing a large *T* on a blank piece of paper and writing "State of Hawaii" on the top part of the *T*; then write similarities in the left column and differences in the right column. Include the URL (this is the http:// address).

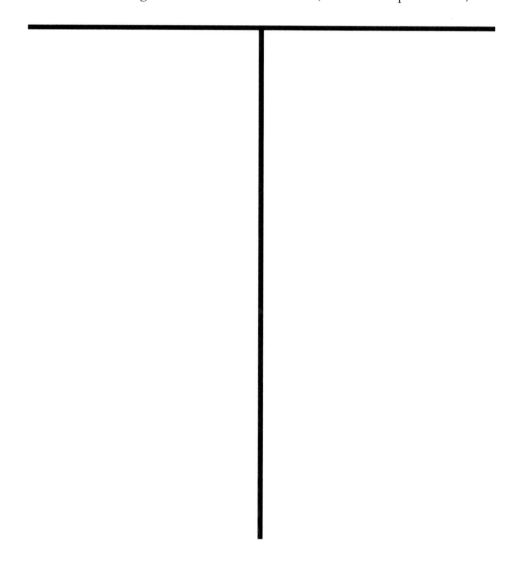

Exercise II

1. Find a classic book from the library, such as Jack London's *The Call of the Wild.* Read the first few pages of the first chapter.

2. Then, find the book online and read the same passage. Classic books are usually available in the public domain for free.

3. Write a reflection on which text was easier to read and why. What are the pros versus cons of reading printed text to its online equivalent?

_____

_____

_____

_____

_____

_____

_____

4. Summarize your findings.

_____

_____

_____

_____

_____

_____

_____

Exercise III

1. Search for online reading speed and comprehension tests. Suggested search engines are Google.com, Bing.com, Yahoo.com, and Ask.com.

2. Follow the directions of the website to determine your level of reading speed online and the amount you comprehend.

3. Print out your results from the web page (if this option is available).

4. Continue to make reading online a priority so you will improve speed and accuracy.

5. Chart your progress throughout the school year by attempting to read more online offerings.

6. Present your findings at the end of the school year or term.

Exercise IV

1. Choose to read something for pleasure online for at least 30 minutes. Select something age-level/grade-level appropriate.

2. At the conclusion of the reading session, write a reflection of what you liked and what you disliked about reading for pleasure from a digital medium.

_____

_____

_____

_____

_____

3. Then, read something in traditional print for at least 30 minutes. At the conclusion of the reading session, write a reflection of what you liked and what you disliked about reading for pleasure from traditional print.

_____

_____

_____

_____

_____

4. It is suggested that you read similar types of material for this exercise.

5. After completing reading both online and in traditional print format, rank your preference between reading online and reading from print. Indicate your reasons why in the space provided.

_____

_____

_____

_____

_____

Exercise V

1. Choose a topic that interests you and read an online story or article for pleasure on that topic.

2. When you are on the web page, notice if there are any advertisements, videos, or other animations displayed on the screen. Make a list of those items you see on the screen (besides the text of the online story or article).

_____

_____

_____

_____

3. Depending on what you listed, did you find any of these other "things" distracting while reading online?

_____

_____

_____

_____

_____

4. Did the online story or article page you were reading from contain any pictures or illustrations? Displays of images or illustrations leave little room for imagination, limiting our ability to form our own mental pictures to illustrate what we are reading. Make a list of what you see on your web page (not including the actual text you are reading).

_____

_____

_____

_____

_____

Unit X Summary

- Reading and using online texts presents many different challenges for students.

- Proper tools and practice can provide a beneficial supplement to sources found in print media.

- The Internet contains a wealth of information—electronic books, research databases, journals, blogs, and other sources widely available free to users.

- Understanding that the Internet is a user-edited phenomenon will help you understand that you must be a discriminating consumer when it comes to text, articles, or facts you find online.

- Practicing using the Internet to read and decipher information will improve your speed and comprehension.

Technology Adaptation

- Create an online account with your school or local library. Download content reading to your smart phone, tablet, computer, or other device. Mix your reading with text and online versions. Over a period of time, determine what reading you prefer by your speed, how much you comprehend, and if you are more likely to read using online or printed texts.

- Check with your local newspaper to see if online subscriptions are free or at a reduced rate to students or schools. Make it a goal to read at least three news stories per day. Choose one of a current national event, one of a current local event, and one article of your choosing. If online newspapers are not available, attempt to do this project using a website such as MSN, *USA Today*, or news from your local radio or television station.

- On your next school project, use the Internet to conduct research using the school or local library. Explore databases with the help of a librarian or teacher.

UNIT XI
USING A DICTIONARY

Challenge! Pre-exercise Activity

The dictionary or an online dictionary is a valuable resource. When you were learning language skills, it was most likely an early reference book that you became familiar with. Since you are already familiar with a dictionary, the challenge will allow you to demonstrate how quickly you can locate and use information from the dictionary.

Word #1

1. _____

2. _____

3. _____

4. _____

5. After dinner tonight, do you want to play a game of cards?

   entry _____ definition _____

Word #2

1. _____

2. _____

3. _____

4. _____

5. Please put the advertisements at eye level so everyone who comes into the store can see them.

   entry _____ definition _____

Word #3

1. _____

2. _____

3. _____

4. _____

The Dictionary: A Complicated Resource

If you had any trouble with the challenge pre-exercise activity, do not worry. This unit will help you to learn more about how to use a dictionary.

Exercise I

Directions: Read sentence 1. If what the sentence says is true for you, put a check in the space before the sentence. Do the same for sentences 2–4. Then answer number 5.

1. _____ I have trouble locating words that I don't know how to spell.

2. _____ I do not use guide words to help locate information.

3. _____ I have difficulty choosing the meaning that fits the context of the sentence.

4. _____ I have difficulty figuring out how a word is pronounced.

5. List any other problems you might have when using a dictionary. _____

_____

_____

_____

_____

Introduction

You may have discovered that using a dictionary can be a frustrating experience. You want to learn about the meaning of a word, so you look it up in the dictionary or access the dictionary using an online dictionary source. But instead of finding one meaning, you find many different ones! What do you do then?

This unit will help you learn how a dictionary is organized and how you can make better use of it.

Exercise II

Directions: Look up the word *run* in your dictionary or access a dictionary using an online source or dictionary alternative. Read through its many meanings. How many different meanings are listed for the word *run*? Write the number of different meanings in the space provided.

_____

Read the following sentences carefully. Find the best definition for the word *run* as it is used in each sentence. Write the correct definition on the line under each sentence.

Example

"Run and call the vet," she ordered. "I can't seem to give her the help she needs with the calf."

1. "I can *run* faster than you," he snarled at me from the starting line.

   _____

2. She had a *run* in her tights.

   _____

3. The dog was not used to his collar and chain. He used to have the *run* of the whole neighborhood.

   _____

4. She decided to *run* for attorney general even though a woman had never held that office before.

   _____

5. Even with the critics' praise, the play only had a three-month *run* on Broadway.

   _____

6. We wait eagerly for the salmon to *run* each year.

   _____

7. His fingers seemed to fly over the clarinet as he played the *runs* in the sonata with ease.

   _____

8. He always liked the Phoenix to Los Angeles *run* with its long stretches of open road.

   _____

9. The motorcycle was *run* off the road by a truck.

   _____

10. The ship's captain wanted to *run* the blockade, but the admiral overruled his command.

_____

Exercise III

Directions: Use a dictionary or access a dictionary using an online source or dictionary alternative. Write the best meaning for the way *trace* is used in each of the following sentences on the line below each sentence.

Example

There are *traces* of poison in the dead man's body.

1. He carefully *traced* the treasure map onto the see-through paper.

_____

2. We found no *traces* of the lost dog.

_____

3. She looked at the old homestead with a *trace* of regret in her eyes.

_____

4. The *trace* from the stem to the leaf carries nitrogen that is needed for photosynthesis.

_____

5. We *traced* the bear tracks to the stream.

_____

6. The lesson was designed to *trace* the rise and the fall of the Roman Empire.

_____

7. She examined the graph that the machine had drawn by measuring his heartbeat. The *traces* showed possible signs of heart weakness.

_____

8. The *traces* snapped, and the frightened horse ran off as the wagon rolled to a bumpy halt.

_____

9. She *traced* her ancestry back to the first Dutch settlers.

_____

10. A tiny *trace* in the watch had broken, stopping the movement of the hour hand.

Unit XI Summary

One word can have many different meanings. You can use the dictionary to learn about the various meanings of a word and to figure out which meanings you need to learn. In today's society, dictionaries are available in print format, online, and in dedicated apps for tablet and mobile devices.

The dictionary can also give you other helpful information about a word:

1. how the word is pronounced;

2. the part or parts of speech of the word;

3. examples of how the word can be used;

4. various forms of the word: for example, plural, past tense, and so on; and

5. any special uses of the word.

Technology Adaptation

- Investigate the many types of dictionaries available to users today: printed format, online, and in dedicated apps for tablets and mobile devices. Find a new and useful dictionary and share findings with the class.

- Conduct an Internet search on the topic of advantages and disadvantages of using an online dictionary. Record and report the findings to classmates.

UNIT XII
IMPROVING YOUR VOCABULARY

Introduction

Your vocabulary includes all of the words that you can understand and use in your thinking, speaking, writing, and reading.

Did you know that the average elementary school student increases his or her vocabulary by about 1,000 words every year? The average junior high or middle school student increases his or her vocabulary by almost 2,000 words each year!

One important way that you learn new words is through your reading. However, when you are reading, there are some problems that you may have in learning about unknown or unfamiliar words.

1. By now, you probably can read quickly enough so that you may skip over words without realizing that you don't understand them.

2. To look up a word in the dictionary, you have to stop reading. This interrupts the flow of your reading.

3. When you use a dictionary, you must be able to choose the correct meaning from all the meanings listed.

This unit will help you to learn ways to solve these problems.

Exercise I

Directions: Your teacher will read the two paragraphs that follow to you. Pay careful attention to the italicized words. Think about the meaning of these words. When your teacher has finished reading, write the definitions of the italicized words on the lines that follow.

Paragraph 1

The day had been a breezy and blue one with lots of sunshine. The sunlight gleamed off the *ridges* of the waves. We tried at first to paddle, but the wind was so strong that it controlled our course. Since our paddling was useless, we *eased* ourselves down and rested against the cushions. We didn't know that sitting on the floor of the canoe was the best thing to do to keep the canoe *upright*.

Paragraph 2

I wish they hadn't been so worried about us. Jeannie and I had only taken the canoe for a quick trip down the lake. As the wind grew stronger and the waves rose higher, the canoe began to rise and fall. We would be about to topple over the *crest* of a wave when our well-*dispersed* weight would balance us. Then we would slide easily down the watery slope. *Peering* over the boat's edge was like looking down from a roller coaster. We were rising and falling with each huge, rolling wave.

ridges _____

eased _____

upright _____

crest _____

dispersed _____

peering _____

Learning about New Words

When you come across an unknown or unfamiliar word in your reading, you can learn its meaning in two ways.

1. You can look up the word in the dictionary, glossary, or thesaurus.

2. You can often figure out the meaning of a new word by looking carefully at the meaning of the words and phrases around it. This is called getting the meaning from *context clues*. Some of you may have used this method in Exercise I.

   A *context* is the setting in which something is found. For example, a museum is a context in which paintings are displayed. A gym is a context in which people play basketball. You expect to find certain things because of the context.

   In language, *context* means the words and sentences around any particular word. *Context clues* are familiar words and phrases in a sentence or paragraph. These are words that you know. From these familiar words, you can often figure out the meaning of an unknown word.

   Example: Many animals are *extinct*, such as dinosaurs.

   extinct means _____

Exercise II

Directions: Read the rest of the story about the canoeing adventure that follows. When you find a word that stops you because you are not sure of its meaning, underline the word.

I didn't worry. Jeannie and I were both strong swimmers. The shore wasn't very far away if the canoe decided to turn us into the foaming waters. I daydreamed that we were sailors on the ocean, conquerors of the deep. Poseidon, with all his power, could not entice us to his kingdom.

The ride finally stopped on the southwest side of the vast lake. The canoe came to a natural halt where the waters lapped gently against a small island. Suddenly we realized that we could never paddle back against those waves.

We would have to wait. The lake would become still toward evening. Jeannie and I climbed out of the canoe and found a healthy patch of blueberries. While we devoured the blueberries, we felt completely carefree. Neither of us realized that we were in big trouble.

Then I spied my uncle. He came in a motorboat. The boat slapped against the waves and sprayed water high into the air. He had come looking for us, probably half expecting the canoe to be capsized with two victims floating facedown beside it. I knew he was relieved that we were alive. I also knew that his relief would soon turn to anger because we had been so foolish and had caused everyone at home to worry. I stood staring at my toes and felt the exhilaration of the day pour out of me.

Exercise III

Directions: On the lines for the new words that follow, write the words that you have underlined in the canoeing story. Then try to figure out the meaning of each word that you have listed from its *context clues*. Write your meaning in the space to the right of the word.

<u>New Words</u>   <u>Meaning</u>

_____   _____

                                  _____

_____   _____

                                  _____

_____   _____

                                  _____

_____   _____

                                  _____

_____   _____

                                  _____

Exercise IV

Directions: Choose the best meaning for the numbered words below from the canoeing story. Mark an *x* on the line in front of the best meaning. Look at the word *vast* below as an example.

Example

vast   a. ___ blue   c. ___ shallow

                      b. ___ far   d. ___ huge

1. devoured   a. ___ ate   c. ___ smashed

                      b. ___ threw around   d. ___ ate hungrily

2. spied   a. ___ looked at   c. ___ spotted

                      b. ___ looked secretly   d. ___ noticed

3. Poseidon   a. ___ a whale   c. ___ god of the sea in Greek mythology

                      b. ___ a king   d. ___ my uncle

4. capsized   a. ___ head size measure   c. ___ turned over

                      b. ___ thrown down   d. ___ collapsed

5. victim   a. ___ someone who is hurt   c. ___ the target or injured

                      b. ___ the weaker one   d. ___ feeling sad

6. relieved   a. ___ replacement   c. ___ jump around

                      b. ___ let go of worry   d. ___ feel a little better

7. exhilaration a. ___ feeling of   c. ___ smashing disappointment

                      b. ___ feeling of sadness d. ___ feeling of great excitement

8. conquerors   a. ___ sailors   c. ___ great boats

                      b. ___ ones who gain control d. ___ captains

How Can You Learn New Words from Your Reading?

1. Keep a special section in your notebook for new words. In this section, write down all the new words that you come across and their meanings.

2. When you come across a word from your reading that you do not fully understand, first try to figure out its meaning from *context clues*.

3. When you cannot figure out the meaning of a new word from its *context clues*, you need to look it up in the dictionary to know what the word means.

Unit XII Summary

A context is the setting in which something is found. In language, *context* means the words and the sentences around any particular word.

Context clues are familiar words and phrases in a sentence or paragraph. From these familiar words, figure out the meaning of an unknown word.

When seeing a new word while reading, first try to figure out its meaning from its context clues. If this is not possible, look it up in the dictionary.

Technology Adaptation

- Use an Internet search engine to locate lists of prefixes, suffixes, and root words.

- Video your advertising jingle and put it on TeacherTube.

TAKING NOTES—MAPPING AND OUTLINING

Introduction

In the unit about reading for meaning, it mentions *mapping* as a way of taking notes. This unit will help you to learn more about how to use *mapping*. It will also help you to learn about another way of taking notes called *outlining*.

Remember: Taking notes helps you to learn more about what you are reading or hearing. Also, when you take notes, you have a record to study when you have a test.

Why Take Notes?

"Taking notes is a lot of work. Why bother?"

Have you ever said this? Or heard a friend say it? Well, why should you take notes? Here are two good reasons for taking notes:

1. When you take notes, you learn by writing the main idea and supporting details down on your paper. You will understand your reading better if you take a few minutes to write or type your notes. You will also remember the main idea and supporting details better. Typing your notes allows you to capture more information than writing notes by hand.

2. When you take notes, you have a record of what you read. You can use the record to study for tests.

Tips for Taking Notes

1. Your notes are for you! Take notes that make sense to you. This means that you can use words from your reading, too, but be sure you understand what your notes say.

2. When you take notes, you don't need to write in complete sentences. Write down only the words and phrases that tell you the main ideas and important details in your reading. You can also use abbreviations and symbols.

3. Don't write down everything in your reading. Write down only the main ideas and important details in your notes.

Breaking Down Sentences

When you take notes, you want to write as few words as possible that tell the important ideas and information. One way to do this is *breaking down* the sentences in your reading into a few key words.

Look at the sentences that follow:

The Hunger Games is a 2008 science fiction novel by the American writer Suzanne Collins. It is written in the voice of 16-year-old Katniss Everdeen, who lives in the nation of Panem in North America.

Now look at an example of the notes from this sentence:

Hunger Games author—Suzanne Collins. Main character—Katniss Everdeen.

When you break down a sentence, try to write as few words as you can. But be sure to keep the important ideas and information.

Exercise I

Directions: Read the sentences that follow. *Break down* each into as few words as possible that tell the important ideas and information.

1. The stories of Greek myths make good reading, for the gods and goddesses are dramatically filled with human emotion: love, hate, and jealousy.

   _____

   _____

2. Energy that was created from wind power could save the states of the windy north from their need to burn fuel.

   _____

   _____

3. The apple, the delicious fruit of the Garden of Eden, is an important fall harvest for the state of New York.

   _____

   _____

4. In the late 1840s many people made a mad dash to California hoping to get rich through the discovery of gold.

   _____

   _____

5. The fair-haired, tall, and hard-fighting sailor of Scandinavia was known as the Viking.

   _____

   _____

Exercise II

Directions: Read the passage about Sioux Indian children. Complete the graphic organizer.

Sioux Indian children were taught to swim at a very early age. When the baby was two months old, its mother would take it to a quiet spot along the riverbank. She would place her hands gently under the baby's belly and place him or her into the shallow, warm water until it came up around him or her. Then suddenly the baby's sturdy legs would begin to kick and his or her arms to whip through the water. The next time the baby lasted a little longer, and by the third or fourth time the mother could take her hands away for a bit while the baby held his or her head up and dogpaddled for himself or herself.

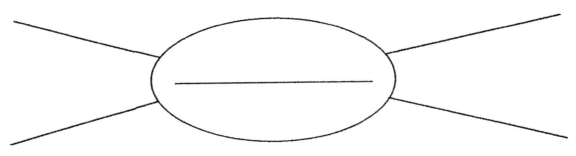

Another Way to Take Notes: Mapping with Numbers

You may have had some difficulty in drawing up your MAP for the paragraph about the Sioux baby. Maybe you asked yourself questions like these: How do I know which line I should start with? Can any detail go on any line? Or is there a place where each one belongs?

When the reading about which you are taking notes is organized in a certain order or sequence, you can still use a kind of *mapping* for your note taking. You do this by numbering the *supporting details* on your *map*. The details show the order of the sequence.

Look at the map that follows, and you will see an example of *mapping with numbers*.

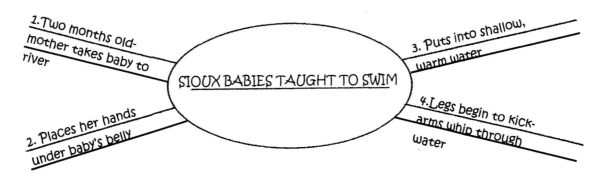

Exercise III

Directions: Try to map the paragraph that follows by *mapping with numbers*.

In its short lifetime, the butterfly goes through four complete changes. We can call these changes "Stages of Life for the Butterfly." The first stage is the egg stage. The adult female chooses a good food source to lay her eggs on. The second stage is the larvae or caterpillar stage. When the eggs hatch, the hungry caterpillars soon devour the leaves around them. They need to eat a lot because they don't eat at all in their third stage, and many don't eat in the fourth stage. Their third stage is spent resting in a cocoon or pupa chrysalis. Finally the adult emerges from the cocoon. In the last stage of life, the butterfly's main job is to mate and lay eggs.

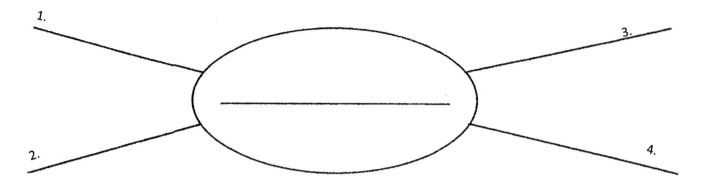

A Third Way to Take Notes: Outlining

When a paragraph is organized into a certain sequence of events, it is easy to use a third way of taking notes called *outlining*. This is much the same as *mapping with numbers*, but the way the information is set up is different.

Following is a form for *outlining*.

Outline Form

    I. Main Idea

        A. Supporting detail

        B. Supporting detail

        C. Supporting detail

How to Outline

1. Use a roman numeral to list main ideas.

2. Use capital letters to list supporting details. Indent each capital letter a little way to the right of the roman numeral.

Exercise IV

Directions: Write your notes about the butterfly in the outline form.

I. _____

   A. _____

   B. _____

   C. _____

   D. _____

Exercise V

Directions: Read the paragraph that follows, and take notes for it on the outline form provided.

What causes hail? If you've ever had to run for cover to escape from the pounding of a hailstorm in the middle of what had been a hot and sticky day in July, you have probably asked yourself the same question. It usually hails in hot weather just before a violent thunderstorm. First cold air gets pushed up above the heavy, warm air. This causes strong upward winds. As it begins to rain, the raindrops are blown upward by these winds. The rain freezes in the cold upper air before it falls to the earth. Each time the droplets fall through the warm air, they gather more moisture. Each time the larger droplets are blown into the cold upper air, they freeze into larger ice balls. When this cycle repeats itself several times, you'll see hail that is the size of golf balls. So hail is created when the raindrops are blown into the colder air over and over again, causing them to freeze into hailstones.

I. _____

   A. _____

   B. _____

   C. _____

   D. _____

   E. _____

How Should *You* Take Notes?

You have tried three different ways of taking notes in this unit: mapping, mapping with numbers, and outlining. All three of these methods can be helpful to you.

Use a way of taking notes that makes sense to you. Experiment with these three ways of taking notes until you find the way that best fits the way that you learn.

You may want to use different note-taking methods at different times. Look carefully at the kind of reading that you're taking notes about. Then decide which way of taking notes will work best for you.

Remember: Your notes are for you! Take notes in your own words that make sense to you.

Cornell Note-Taking Guide

There are four easy steps in taking notes in this manner.

a. Draw a line vertically on the left side of a piece of paper.

b. Write important information from the lecture or text in the column on the right side of the paper.

c. After notes are completed, review the notes and write questions from the content in the margin on the left side of the paper.

d. Cover the right column, exposing only the questions on the left. Self-quiz or work with other students to learn the important concepts.

Use one of your textbooks and complete a Cornell note-taking guide. Use the form in the workbook, another sheet of paper, or complete one electronically.

Knowledge Chart

There are six steps in completing this strategy.

a. Locate a text or visual images to share.

b. Using a piece of paper, divide it vertically into two columns of equal size.

c. At the top of the column on the left, write "Prior Knowledge." At the top of the column on the right, write "Need to Remember."

d. Prior to reading the assigned text, brainstorm what you already know about the topic and record the information in the column under "Prior Knowledge."

e. After reading the passage, list in the "Need to Remember" column notes from the text. Continue until you have listed several pieces of important information.

f. Using the information from both columns, work individually or in small groups to formulate questions for what you would still like to learn about the topic.

Use one of your textbooks and complete a knowledge chart. Use the form in the workbook, another sheet of paper, or complete one electronically.

Text Structure Strategy

To use the text structure strategy, follow the directions that follow.

a. Remember that authors use the structure of a text to facilitate understanding. If you do not understand the significance of these features or how to use them advantageously, you may have difficulty focusing, monitoring, and understanding written material.

b. Divide notebook paper into three equal vertical columns. Write "Text Structure" at the top of the column on the left, and write "Example" at the top of the middle column. Write "How It Helps" at the top of the column on the right side of the paper.

c. Complete the organizer by locating the specific support, giving an example of the support, and explaining how the support helps with comprehension. Sample supports include but are not limited to the following:

- chapter title

- headings

- subheadings

- photos

- bold print

- italics

- diagrams

- graphic organizers

- author questions

- key vocabulary

Use one of your textbooks and complete a text structure organizer. Use the form in the workbook, another sheet of paper, or complete one electronically.

Unit XIII Summary

There are several good ways of taking notes: outlining, mapping, mapping with numbers, Cornell note taking, knowledge chart, and text structure.

Outlining

    I. Main Idea

        A. Supporting detail

        B. Supporting detail

        C. Supporting detail

        D. Supporting detail

Mapping

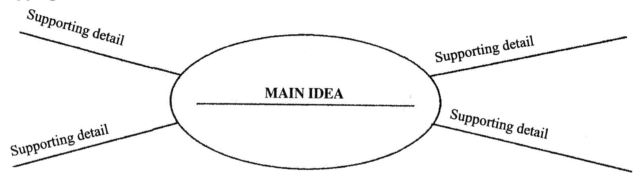

Mapping with Numbers

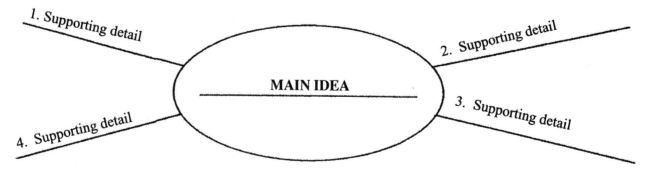

Technology Adaptation

- Use an Internet search engine to find other graphic organizers that can be used for taking notes.

- Use the open-source program FreeMind to make additional mind maps.

CORNELL NOTES

Questions	Notes
	Summary

KNOWLEDGE CHART

Prior Knowledge	Need to Remember

TEXT STRUCTURE

Text Structure	Example	How It Helps

UNIT XIV
LISTENING AND TAKING NOTES

Introduction

Learning in school is accomplished in a number of ways. Listening carefully during a class discussion or while a teacher lectures can be enhanced by taking notes. While this program will teach you to take notes in a variety of forms, this unit will give you practice in listening and taking notes.

Listening and Taking Notes

Much of what you need to learn to do well in any class will be covered in the class itself. One way to learn more in class is to take notes.

Taking *brief* notes in class can help you learn in the following ways:

1. Taking notes in class can help you to find the main ideas of what is being said, because you will only want to write down the main ideas.

2. Writing down the main ideas as notes will help you to learn them better.

3. When you take notes in class, you can use your notes later to study for a test.

How Do You Start?

Before you start to take notes from listening, decide which note-taking method best fits your way of learning. At first, use the method with which you are most comfortable, the one that seems the easiest for you.

Once you feel comfortable with one note-taking method, try using others. You may want to follow these suggestions:

1. You can use the *outline* method for any kind of organized talk. In an organized talk, the speaker has put the main ideas and important details into an order to share with you. Sometimes your teacher will put an *outline* on the board at the beginning of class or during class. Use this *outline* as a starting point for your *outline* notes.

2. You can also use the *mapping with numbers* method for an organized talk.

3. You can use the *mapping* method or the *mapping with numbers* method for taking notes during any activity that is less organized, such as a class discussion or question period.

4. The knowledge chart works well for class discussions. Just don't forget to brainstorm prior to the discussion what you already know about the topic.

5. The Cornell note-taking method works well for vocabulary words, taking notes from a text, or writing notes during a class discussion or lecture.

Tips for Taking Notes from Listening

1. Be an *active* listener! Try to make sense of what the speaker is saying. Try to connect what the speaker is saying with what you already know.

2. If you can, "picture" in your mind what is being said.

3. Before you start to take notes, think about how the speaker has organized what he or she will say. For example, is there an outline on the board? Is it a class discussion? Then decide what method you want to use to take notes.

4. Try to spend most of your time listening. Figure out what the main ideas are, and write them down. Use only words and phrases, not complete sentences. *Remember:* your notes are for you; make sure they make sense to you!

5. When your teacher tells you that you will need to know something, be sure to write it down.

Exercise I

Directions: Your teacher will give a talk for a few minutes. Take notes from the talk in the space below.

_____

_____

_____

_____

_____

_____

_____

_____

_____

_____

_____

Looking at Your Notes

Directions: Look carefully at your notes from Exercise I. Then answer the questions that follow.

1. What note-taking method did you use? _____

    _____

2. How well did this method work for you? _____

    _____

3. Do your notes make sense to you? _____

    _____

4. How could you make your notes better or more helpful to you? _____

    _____

Exercise II

Directions: Your teacher will lead a short class discussion. Take notes from the discussion in the space that follows.

_____

_____

_____

_____

_____

_____

_____

_____

_____

_____

_____

_____

Looking Again at Your Notes

Directions: Look carefully at your notes from Exercise II. Then answer the questions below.

1. Did you use the same note-taking method that you used for Exercise I?

_____

_____

2. Explain why you chose the method that you used.

_____

_____

_____

_____

3. How is taking notes during a class discussion different from taking notes during a lecture?

_____

_____

_____

_____

4. Do your notes make sense to you?

_____

_____

_____

_____

5. How could you make your notes better or more helpful to you?

_____

_____

_____

_____

Unit XIV Summary

Much of what you need to learn for any class will be covered in the class itself. Taking *brief* notes in class can help you with this learning.

Use a note-taking method with which you are comfortable when you start. Later on, you may want to use different methods in different situations. For example:

1. You can use the *outline* method for any kind of organized talk. You can also use *mapping with numbers* for an organized talk.

2. You can use the *mapping* method or *mapping with numbers* for taking notes during a less organized activity, such as a class discussion.

Be an *active* listener! Try to make sense of what the speaker is saying. Spend most of your time listening. Figure out what the main ideas are, and write them down in words and phrases.

Remember: Your notes are for you. Take notes that make sense to you.

Technology Adaptation

- Choose a partner and pick a note-taking strategy to practice. Listen to an audio book or a podcast and take notes. Compare the notes with your partner.

UNIT XV
PUTTING A BOOK TOGETHER/TEXT FEATURES

Introduction

Almost every textbook has many different parts other than just the *body* or *text* of the book, that is, the written sections in each chapter. Most of your textbooks have all of the parts listed below:

- title page and copyright page

- table of contents

- body or text

- glossary

- index

- bibliography

When you know how to find and use all of these parts, your textbook can become more helpful to you in your learning.

In this unit, you will learn about the different parts of a textbook by putting a book together. The *body* of the "book" you will put together is actually an article called "Monkey Business."

Exercise I

Directions: *Survey* the article "Monkey Business."

Title Page and Copyright Page

The *title page* is the very beginning of a book. The *title page* tells you the title of the book. It also lists the author and publisher and where the book was published.

The *copyright page* is usually right after the title page. This page tells you who has the right to print the book and when the book was first printed.

Exercise II

Directions:

A. Find the *title page* in this study skills program, and locate the following information:

  • What is the title of this book? Who is the author? Who published the book? Where was the book published?

B. Find the *copyright page* of this book. Locate the following information:

  • Who has the right to print this book? When was this book first printed?

C. Using the title page and copyright page in this book as a source of information and as a model, make up a *title page* for "Monkey Business."

_____

_____

_____

_____

Table of Contents

The *table of contents* tells you what you will find inside the book. It lets you know about the main ideas that are covered in the book. The *table of contents* also tells you how many chapters there are in the book and on what page each chapter begins.

You can find the *table of contents* in the front of the book, usually right after the copyright page.

Exercise III

Directions:

A. Find the *table of contents* in this study skills program, and examine it.

B. Read over the article "Monkey Business." Decide what the chapter headings should be, and make a list of these headings.

C. Create a *table of contents* for "Monkey Business." Your table of contents should contain chapter titles and pages on which the chapters begin.

_____

_____

_____

_____

Glossary

The *glossary* of a textbook is a lot like a dictionary for that book. It lists words that are new or unfamiliar to most readers and tells you how the words are pronounced, what part of speech they are, and what their meanings are.

The *glossary* covers meanings that are used within that book. It often does not list every meaning of a word as a dictionary would.

You can usually find the *glossary* at the end of the body of the book.

Exercise IV

Directions:

A. Read the article "Monkey Business."

B. There are 17 underlined words or terms in the body of "Monkey Business." Find all of these words or terms; make a list of them, and put the list into alphabetical order.

PLEASE NOTE! A term is a group of words that have a particular meaning together. Some of the terms in "Monkey Business" are *animal behaviorists*, *endangered species*, and *hurdy-gurdy man*.

In a *glossary*, terms like these are listed as if they were a single word.

_____

_____

_____

_____

C. Using context clues or a dictionary, write a glossary definition for each underlined word or term in the body of the article. Be sure to use the same meaning that is used in "Monkey Business."

_____

_____

_____

_____

_____

_____

_____

_____

D. Put your words and definitions together so you have a *glossary* for "Monkey Business."

_____

_____

_____

_____

_____

_____

_____

_____

Index

An *index* lists specific names and ideas found within a book. This list is in alphabetical order. Numbers of the pages where ideas and names can be found are listed after the names and ideas.

You can usually find the *index* at the very back of the book. Some reference books have a separate volume for the index.

Exercise V

Directions:

A. All of the words and terms in the list that follows appear in the article "Monkey Business." Put this list of words and terms into alphabetical order.

Pre-monkey	Tree shrew	Bushbaby
Tarsier	New World monkeys	Old World monkeys
Proboscis monkey	Spider monkey	Hurdy-gurdy man
Monkeys as pets	Zoos	Endangered species
Colobus monkey	Guenons	Woolly monkey
Howler monkey	Uakari	Langur
Macaque	Owl monkey	Marmoset
Mangabeys		

_____   _____

_____   _____

_____   _____

_____   _____

_____   _____

_____   _____

_____   _____

B. Read the article "Monkey Business." As you read, locate the words from the previous list in the body of the article. Each time that you find a word in the body of the article, write that page number after the word in the list.

Make sure you find each time that each word appears.

C. Put all of the words and page numbers together, so you have an index for "Monkey Business."

Bibliography

A *bibliography* is a list of references that an author has used to help him or her write a book or article. References can include books or articles. A *bibliography* lists the references alphabetically by the author's last name.

A *bibliography* is set up in the following way: Author's last name, First name. *Title.* Place published: Name of publisher, Date published.

You can usually find the *bibliography* just before the index at the back of the book.

Exercise VI

Directions:

Arrange the references for "Monkey Business" listed in correct alphabetical order.

Write a *bibliography* for "Monkey Business." Be sure to punctuate everything correctly.

Whitlock, Ralph, *Chimpanzees.* Milwaukee: Raintree Children's Books, 1977. Morris, Dean. *Monkeys and Apes.* Milwaukee: Raintree Children's Books, 1977. Shuttlesworth, Dorothy. *Monkeys, Great Apes, and Small Apes.* Garden City, NY: Doubleday and Company, Inc., 1972. Leen, Nina. *Monkeys.* New York: Holt, Rinehart, and Winston, 1976. Annixter, Jane, and Paul Annixter. *Monkeys and Apes.* New York: Franklin Watts, 1976.

_____

_____

_____

_____

_____

_____

_____

_____

_____

Monkey Business

Introduction: A Brief History

At zoos, people often find themselves standing in front of monkey cages. They stare at the intelligent animals that seem curiously like humans. Monkeys can use simple tools, and their hands twist and turn cleverly. Monkeys even seem to have emotions. Actually, monkeys are like humans in another way. They both belong to the same group of _mammals_, as do chimpanzees and apes. This group is called _primates_. All primates have grasping hands or feet, well-developed vision, and relatively large brains.

The primate story began many millions of years ago. A "pre-monkey" known as the _tree shrew_ made its appearance on the earth about 70 million years ago. It preferred the high treetops where it could look down safely on the giants we know as dinosaurs. It was one of the first mammals. Since it was so tiny, the _tree shrew_ was timid. It preferred hiding to fighting. Its clever, long fingers, a brain that was large for its size, and its ability in climbing made the tree shrew a survivor. It still lives today, long after the dinosaurs, on the island of Madagascar (a large island off the eastern coast of Africa).

tree shrew

bushbaby

tarsier

The tree shrew, the _bushbaby_, and the _tarsier_ are some of the animals we call "pre-monkeys." They are like monkeys in many ways, but they aren't as highly developed as monkeys are.

Notice the huge, staring eyes. Unlike "real" monkey's eyes, these eyes cannot move within their sockets.

The first of the "real" monkeys emerged about 30 million years ago. Unlike the "pre-monkey," monkeys have eyes that move in their sockets, arms and legs more useful for speedy climbing and running, hands better developed for holding, and a larger and more complicated brain.

Two Classifications

Monkeys come in all sizes, shapes, and colors. But they fit into two large _classifications_ or categories. These classifications are Old World monkeys and New World monkeys. They are put into these classifications because of where they are found. Old World monkeys are found in the rain forests of Africa and Asia. They are also found in the islands off these _continents_. New World monkeys are found in the rain forests of South America and Central America. A few can even be found in Mexico. There are many noticeable differences between these two kinds of monkeys.

Old World Monkeys

Old World monkeys are generally considered to have more intelligence than New World monkeys. They will often use simple tools, such as a stick for digging out delicious ants or a rock for killing small game. Their noses are more like human noses than those of New World monkeys are. They are narrow and point downward.

Old World monkeys have 32 teeth, the same as humans have. They have tough protective pads under their _haunches_.

At one time, _animal behaviorists_, scientists who study animal behavior, thought that Old World monkeys were more disagreeable than New World monkeys; Old World monkeys were believed to be more dangerous as they fiercely guarded their _territories_. Modern animal behaviorists disagree. They point to the poor conditions under which the first studies were made. The monkeys were kept in small cages, were not fed proper foods, and often were teased. No wonder the monkeys appeared to be fierce!

New World Monkeys

New World monkeys often have a long and agile tail; most Old World monkeys do not. This tail can be used as another hand for grasping and swinging. These tails are called _prehensile_ because of their grasping qualities.

The New World monkeys have broad and round noses. They rely on _instinct_ for survival. They rarely use tools as Old World monkeys do. Their bodies are generally longer and slimmer. This makes climbing and traveling through the trees easier. Almost all New World monkeys live in trees. Some Old World monkeys get too heavy to feel comfortable staying high up in the air on slender branches.

Proboscis Monkey

Proboscis means long-nosed in Latin. The bright-red head and the long nose of the adult proboscis make it one of the strangest-looking creatures in the animal world. The adult male's nose can reach three inches below its chin. Scien-

Proboscis monkey watching from his tree top.

115

tists believe this nose could be the sounding board for the long drawn out "honk" or "keehonk" of the proboscis. The proboscis lives in the rain forests of Borneo, an island in the western Pacific Ocean, and travels through the trees in large, noisy troops.

The proboscis is an example of an Old World monkey. It may weigh less than a pound at birth, but when full grown, the male can weigh up to fifty pounds. The female weighs about twenty-five pounds. The proboscis does not have sunken eyes like many monkeys. Its eyes are small, and it seems to look out intelligently. A baby proboscis's nose will start out looking much like any other monkey's nose. As the monkey matures, the nose grows, and the lips draw into a smile. It's almost as if the proboscis knows what a strange-looking character it is!

The proboscis eats large amounts of leaves. It also enjoys shoots from mangoes and other fruit. However, it is not an overworked monkey, constantly on the lookout for food. It eats when it wants to. It usually prefers to spend its time lounging on its back or sitting motionless among the tree leaves. The proboscis also enjoys an occasional swim in a tropical river or lake.

Hunters value the proboscis monkey for its rust-colored fur. This is one reason why the proboscis is on the _endangered species_ list.

Proboscis male—his nose can be three inches longer than his chin!

Spider Monkey

One of the most common New World monkeys is the spider monkey. This monkey gets its name because of its "spider-like" appearance as it moves through the trees at remarkable speeds. Its prehensile or grasping tail helps it to be quick and agile. It uses its tail to climb high into the rain forests of South and Central America and Mexico. The tail can also help the spider monkey grab bits of food as it stretches down from the trees. The end of the tail has a patch of bare skin that is very sensitive. It can pick up a small fruit or a peanut.

The spider monkey usually travels in small bands or groups. However, up to thirty spider monkeys have been seen traveling together. Their voices cut through the rain forest in a high-pitched warning yelp. This sounds a lot like many barking terriers.

One of the spider monkey's favorite sports is wrestling. It does not like to swim, even though experiments have shown that it can swim quite well. The spider monkey prefers to hook its long tail on a branch and swing back and forth like a hammock.

The spider monkey is the monkey we picture traveling with the _hurdy-gurdy man_. The traveling musician would play his wind-up organ on the street as his spider monkey begged for coins.

Spider monkey reaching for delicate bits.

"Hurdy-gurdy" man and his trained monkey.

Monkeys in Captivity

Monkeys do not usually adapt very well as pets. They seem quite happy and sweet when they are young but often grow up to be moody and unpredictable. They bite and spit at times and do cute tricks at other times.

Zoos keep many types of monkeys. These monkeys adapt very well if they have large, clean cages, which also have equipment for climbing and swinging.

Besides having monkeys for people to watch, zoos want to help any monkeys that are an endangered species. Monkeys are hunted for food, fur, pets, and medical research. Also, each year more and more acres of rain forest are being cut down by farmers and builders. Monkey populations all over the world are on the *decline*. Since monkeys *breed*, or reproduce their young, very well in captivity, a well-kept zoo is an important place for them.

Some information about the kinds of monkeys you might find in a zoo is listed below.

Type of Monkey	Zoo Life Span	Home Continent
Colobus monkey	8–12 years	Africa
Guenons	20–30 years	Africa
Howler monkey	10–15 years	Central, South America
Langur	10–20 years	Asia
Macaque	25–30 years	Asia
Mangabeys	15–20 years	Africa
Marmoset	2–8 years	South America
Owl monkey	10–13 years	Central, South America
Proboscis monkey	4–10 years	Asia
Spider monkey	17–20 years	South, Central America
Uakari	5–9 years	South America
Woolly monkey	10–12 years	South America

If you go to a zoo, stand in front of the monkey cage and try to imagine being in the rain forests of South America, Central America, Africa, or Asia. Do not be surprised if you think you see a monkey look right at you and then seem to be laughing. The monkey may just think humans are strange-looking creatures!

Exercise VII

Directions: Answer the questions below, using the table of contents, the glossary, the index, and the bibliography that you have put together for "Monkey Business."

1. By looking at the table of contents, can you tell if this book will inform you about what monkeys eat? How do you know?

   _____

   _____

2. Use the glossary to help you answer this question: Can you give an example of an *instinct*?

   _____

   _____

3. Use the index to help you answer this question: What is unusual about the "pre-monkey's" eyes?

_____

_____

4. Use the bibliography to help you answer this question: Which book is the most recent source of information for "Monkey Business"?

_____

_____

Exercise VIII

Directions: Answer the questions below, using the parts of the article "Monkey Business" that you have put together. Then, in the marked space, write which part(s) of the book you used to help you answer the question.

Example

What chapter would you read if you wanted to learn about how monkeys live in zoos?

_____

Part of the book: _____

1. Are you a mammal? Name three kinds of mammals.

_____

_____

Part of the book: _____

2. Where does the spider monkey live?

_____

_____

Part of the book: _____

3. Where are Raintree Children's Books published?

_____

_____

Part of the book: _____

4. What kind of question might you ask an animal behaviorist about your pet dog?

_____

_____

Part of the book: _____

5. Are monkeys good pets? Why or why not?

_____

_____

Part of the book: _____

6. Where would you find a description of the Proboscis monkey?

_____

_____

Part of the book: _____

Unit XV Summary

You can use your textbooks better to help you learn when you understand how the parts of a book fit together. Also, when you want to find out specific information, knowing the parts of a textbook and how to use them can save you time and effort.

The main parts of a textbook are these:

1. The *title page* tells you the title of the book. It also tells you the author, the publisher, and where the book was published.

2. The *copyright page* tells you who owns the right to print the book and when the book was first printed.

3. The *table of contents* informs you what the chapters are in the book and on what page each one starts. It can also help you to find out what main ideas are covered within the book.

4. The *body* or *text* of the book includes all of the written sections in each chapter.

5. The *glossary* is like a dictionary for new or unfamiliar words used in the book. Words in a glossary are listed in alphabetical order; each listing tells you the meaning of that word as it is used in the book.

6. The *index* is an alphabetical listing of specific names and ideas found within a book. Numbers of the pages where the names and ideas can be found are listed after the names and ideas.

7. The *bibliography* lists all of the references, the books and articles that the author has used in writing the book.

Technology Adaptation

- Note the features of an online text/article. How is the format of an online text different from a traditional text?

- Use a search engine to look for different online resources for making bibliographies and citations.

UNIT XVI
STUDYING AND TEST TAKING

Introduction: Studying—Finding the Right Environment

Studying means learning. When you are studying to be a musician, a carpenter, or a soccer player, you need the right *environment* for your learning. The *environment* is everything that surrounds you. For example, when you are learning to play a musical instrument, you need a quiet place where you can hear what you are playing and where no one will bother you.

When you are studying for school, you also need the right *study environment*. The first part of this unit will help you to think about what kind of *study environment* is good for you and the way you learn. It will also give you a few suggestions for how you might make better use of your study time.

Exercise I

Directions: Read the paragraphs, and follow the instructions listed.

Suzanne's teacher spent the first few days of school talking about the conditions in a good study or learning environment. He said that people have different learning styles and so different people learn best in different kinds of *study environments*. He wanted all of his students to experiment with different *study environments* and find out what helped them to learn better.

Suzanne tried many different conditions before she found the environment that was best for her. Her two most different experiments are in pictures that follow.

Look at the pictures of Suzanne's two study environments. Then, on the lines that follow, write down all the differences you see.

Environment #1

Environment #2

Environment #1	Environment #2
_____	_____
_____	_____
_____	_____
_____	_____
_____	_____
_____	_____
_____	_____
_____	_____

Exercise II

Directions: Look at both of the lists you have made. Circle all of the conditions in both lists that would distract or bother *you* if you were trying to learn.

Now make a list on the lines that follow of what you would want in an environment that would help you study.

_____

_____

_____

_____

Tips for Studying

1. Each person seems to have good times of the day for learning. When do you learn best? In the morning, the afternoon, or the evening? Try to figure out when is the best time for you to study.

2. When you study at home, ask your family to help you by keeping things fairly quiet.

3. Get a small notebook to write down what you have to do for homework. Before you leave school, check your notebook. Then ask yourself, "What will I need to take home tonight?" Make sure you take everything you need home with you.

4. Have your materials together when you start to study. Ask yourself, "Do I need a pencil and paper? A dictionary? Anything else?"

5. How long can you pay attention when you are doing your schoolwork? Experiment to find out. If you can concentrate for fifteen or twenty minutes, plan to study for that long. Then do something active and fun for a few minutes before you start studying again.

6. Each time that you plan to study, set goals for yourself. These goals should be things that you can really do in the time you have. For example, you may not be able to read an entire book for a book report. Instead, decide how many chapters you can read, and try to reach your goal.

How Do You Learn?

Some people learn best when they *hear* information. Others learn best by *writing* important details. Sometimes *picturing the facts* is a good way to learn. Another way to learn is to *try to connect* or make sense of how facts fit together. Most of us learn by combining these ways.

When you pay attention to how you learn best, you will be able to learn more effectively.

Exercise III: Part A

Directions: You will experiment to see how you learn the best. Look at the chart called "Facts about the First Five American Presidents." You will have five minutes to try to memorize the facts. Then you will be asked to fill in the blanks on a similar chart.

Think about ways that you learn the best. Try some of the following ways:

1. Say the facts aloud to yourself.

2. Study the lists. Then cover the lists and see if you can remember the information.

3. Write the facts on another piece of paper.

4. Think of the facts in a way that makes sense to you. For example: Of the first five American presidents, three of them were Democratic-Republican. Each of the first five presidents, except for John Adams, had eight years in office. James Monroe was famous for the Monroe Doctrine.

Facts about the First Five American Presidents

NAME	WHEN ELECTED	PARTY	FAMOUS FOR
George Washington	1789	None	First president
			General in the Revolution
John Adams	1797	Federalist	Helped write the Declaration of Independence
			First president to live in Washington
Thomas Jefferson	1801	Democratic-Republican	Author of Declaration of Independence
			Scientist farmer
			Architect
James Madison	1809	Democratic-Republican	Founder of Constitution
			Husband of Dolly
			Wrote 9 amendments
James Monroe	1817	Democratic-Republican	Hero of the Revolution
			Monroe Doctrine

Exercise III: Part B

Directions: See how many facts you remember. Fill in the blank spaces that follow. When you have finished, turn back to the previous chart and check your answers.

Remember: This is an experiment to see how you learn; this is not a test. It is more important to recognize how you learn than to pay attention to how many facts you remember.

Facts about the First Five American Presidents

NAME	WHEN ELECTED	PARTY	FAMOUS FOR
1. _____	1789	None	First president
			2. _____
			_____
John Adams	3. _____	Federalist	4. Helped write the
			_____
			_____
			First president to live in Washington
5. _____	1801	Democratic-Republican	Author of Declaration of Independence
			6. _____
			Architect
James Madison	7. _____	8. _____	9. Founder of the
		_____	_____
			10. Husband of
			_____
			11. Wrote __ amendments
12. _____	1817	Democratic-Republican	13. Hero of the
			_____
			14. _____ Doctrine

Exercise IV

Directions: Look at the statements that follow. Check the statements that apply to you.

1. ____ I learn facts best by writing them.

2. ____ I learn facts best when I see them in lists and memorize what the lists look like.

3. ____ I learn facts best when I say them aloud.

4. ____ I learn facts best by combining 1–3.

5. ____ I have a difficult time memorizing facts, but I can remember facts when I see how they all fit together.

Introduction: Test Taking

When you put your time and effort into studying for a test, you want to do well. To do that, you need to learn the material that the test covers. You can also do better on tests if you understand how to answer the different kinds of questions. This part of the unit will suggest some tips you can use with five different types of questions:

1. true/false questions

2. multiple-choice questions

3. short-answer questions

4. matching questions

5. fact/opinion questions

True/False Questions

True/false questions are statements that you are asked to judge whether they are true or false?

Tips for True/False Questions

1. Read the question carefully. If *any part* of the statement is false, then it is a false statement. Mark it false.

2. Watch for "key words" like the ones listed. Think about what these words mean in the statement; they can help you make a decision.

always	all	never
only	usually	often
frequently		

Exercise V

Directions: Read the statements that follow. Decide whether each statement is true or false. Mark a *T* for true or an *F* for false in the space after each statement.

   1. All people who live in Norway have blond hair. _____

   2. Mercury, Venus, Jupiter, Mars, and Earth's moon are planets within our solar system. _____

   3. All even numbers can be divided evenly by two. _____

   4. Plants never grow unless they get direct sunlight. _____

   5. A calm always comes before a thunderstorm. _____

   6. Animals usually have their young in the spring. _____

Multiple-Choice Questions

Multiple-choice questions ask you to choose the right answer from a group of possible answers.

Tips for Multiple-Choice Questions

   1. Read the question carefully. Then see if you know the answer to the question *before* you even look at the choices.

   2. Read all of the choices given, and pick the *best* answer. Some questions give two or more answers that are right in some way. You need to pick the one that is the *best* answer.

   3. Be sure to read *all* of the choices given, even if the first or second one seems right. They may all be correct, and the last choice may be "all of the above."

   4. If you do not know which answer is right, cross out all of the ones that you know are *wrong*. Then pick the best answer from the remaining choices. If you don't know which one is best, make a good guess.

   5. You should always put down an answer on a multiple-choice question, even if it's a guess, unless your teacher tells you not to guess.

Exercise VI

Directions: Answer each of the questions that follow by writing the letter of the correct answer in the blank at the right.

1. The word *watch* means: _____

    (A) a timing device

    (B) to look at something closely

    (C) a duty on a ship

    (D) all of the above

2. Railroads played an important role in American history because _____

    (A) they transported all of the country's supplies

    (B) they never broke down

    (C) they were often smelly, so people started taking airplanes

    (D) they provided efficient transportation for people and supplies

3. When Columbus set sail in 1492 _____

    (A) the earth wasn't round

    (B) all people believed that the earth wasn't round

    (C) Columbus believed that the earth was round

    (D) almost all of the sailors believed that the earth was round

4. Bats are unlike most mammals because they _____

    (A) never eat eels

    (B) have body temperature changes

    (C) cannot learn to read and write

    (D) hibernate in the summer when it is the coldest

Short-Answer Questions

Short-answer questions ask you to write in the correct answer as part of a statement. They are also called "fill-in-the-blank" questions.

Tips for Short-Answer Questions

1. Read the question carefully. Ask yourself: What is this question asking? Then write in the answer if you know it.

2. If you do not know the exact answer but do know something that is related to it, write down what you *do* know. You may get partial credit for it.

3. If you don't know the correct answer but have an idea about it, make a good guess!

Exercise VII

Directions: Read the statements that follow. Fill in the best answer you know.

1. There are _____ months of the year that begin with the letter *J*.

2. The sixth American president was _____.

3. The three states of matter are gas, solid, and _____.

4. The author of *The Chronicles of Narnia* is _____.

5. The United States is bordered by two other countries. The northern border country is _____. The southern border country is _____.

Matching Questions

Matching questions usually give you two lists of information and ask you to match things on one list with things on the other.

Tips for Matching Questions

1. Match the easiest things first, the ones you know most about.

2. When you have matched an item, cross out its number or letter, so you know you've already done it.

3. If you are not sure about any of the items, make a good guess!

Exercise VIII

Directions: Read the two lists below. Write the number of the piece of sports equipment in the blank before the sport for which you'd use the equipment.

a. _____ baseball   1. shoulder pads

b. _____ football   2. hoop

c. _____ basketball   3. foil

d. _____ field hockey   4. paddle

e. _____ table tennis   5. mallet

f. _____ polo   6. hockey stick

g. _____ fencing   7. bat

Fact/Opinion Questions

A *fact* is a statement that can be proven to be true or false. An *opinion* is a belief. A belief cannot be proven.

Look at the question below:

The United States did not pass the Nineteenth Amendment, which gave women the right to vote, until 1920 because:

   a. men still wanted women at home to cook and raise families

   b. women were not politically wise enough

   c. in those times women were not as intelligent as men

   d. it took over forty years for enough states to pass the Nineteenth Amendment.

Although you might agree with some of the first three choices, they are really *opinions* and not *facts*. Usually true/false, multiple-choice, and short-answer questions are looking for *facts* and not *opinions*.

Another kind of question asks you to identify statements as *fact* or *opinion*. It is important to know that opinions are not wrong. Opinions can be supported by facts.

Tips for Finding Facts

   1. Facts usually explain who, what, where, or why.

   2. Facts can be found in a reference book such as a dictionary, an encyclopedia, an atlas, and so on.

   3. Facts are either true or false.

4. The following words are usually *not* found in factual statements.

should   maybe   could have been

if   should be   probably

Exercise IX

Directions: Read the statements that follow. Decide whether they are facts or opinions. Write an *O* after the statements that are opinions and an *F* after the statements that are facts.

1. Children should be seen and not heard. _____

2. The United States had thirteen original states. _____

3. Dancers have a deep appreciation for music. _____

4. George Washington was an officer in the Continental Army. _____

5. The United States could have been the first country in outer space if more money were given to space exploration in the 1950s. _____

6. Abraham Lincoln walked three miles to school. _____

7. The earth will probably have a significant climate change in the next ten years. _____

8. All people should have a right to equal education. _____

Unit XVI Summary

Your *study environment* can have a lot to do with how well you learn. Find out what kind of study environment works best for you. Then do your studying in that kind of environment.

When you understand how different kinds of questions work, you can often do better on tests.

1. True/false questions: If the answer is only partly false, mark it false. Watch out for "key words" like *always*, *never*, or *only*. These words can help you decide whether a statement is true or false.

2. Multiple-choice questions: Read the question, and see if you know the answer before you look at the choices. Then read all the choices, and pick the *best* answer. If you're not sure about the answer, cross out the choices that are wrong. Then choose the best remaining answer. Make a good guess!

3. Short-answer questions: Read the statement carefully. If you do not know the exact answer, write down the best answer you can think of.

4. Matching questions: Match the items you know first. Then cross them out. Make a good guess about the remaining items.

5. Fact /opinion questions: It is important to be able to tell fact from opinion. Multiple-choice questions and true/false questions are usually looking for facts and not opinions. You can recognize facts as short bits of information that you can locate in a reference book. There are also "key words" that help you decide what are not facts, such as *should be*, *probably*, and *may be*.

Technology Adaptation

- Create an electronic poster with study tips that work for you to share with other students in the class.

- Choose three things you have learned in this unit and post them to a class blog to share so others may learn from your findings.

- Create quizzes on sites such as www.onlinequizcreator.com. Design questions that assess your comprehension of the five different kinds of questions in this unit.

MULTIMEDIA PRESENTATIONS

Introduction

The use of technology makes learning a more visual and interactive process. Everyone can be creative, and the Internet and commercial software allow users the ability to do just about anything when it comes to delivering a multimedia presentation. Software standards like PowerPoint and Internet presentation tools like Prezi and PowToon allow you to make things fun while giving information at the same time. For enhanced video-heavy presentations, try Animoto and MovieMaker, or create a channel on websites like Vimeo. Still yet, photos may be manipulated using commercial products like Photoshop while free applications like PicMonkey do similar things in just a few clicks—and without cost to the user.

Multimedia presentations using electronic delivery methods allow users to share information in interesting formats. Further, it allows you to be creative and engaged. Traditional presentation resources only allowed users to present words and pictures, information given in silos rather than blended together. Now you have the ability to make a fully interactive presentation, complete with text and information, photos, videos, and graphics. Presentations may be shared with the intended audience, or presentations may be shared via the Internet and distributed to virtually any audience.

Step 1: Explore different commercial presentation software and presentation applications using the web. Choose from a list of topics related to the given lesson and prepare an original presentation.

Step 2: Using the same presentation previously prepared, incorporate at least three pictures or graphics to enhance the presentation. The pictures/graphics should be modified for effect using one of the example programs listed, or you may choose to use a different product with teacher approval. The pictures/graphics should enhance the project and provide focus and clarity to the intended audience.

Step 3: Using the same presentation previously prepared, incorporate at least a two-minute motion-picture segment. Choose two to four movie clips to support the topic and include at least two minutes of video in the presentation. If video camera equipment is available, make a movie for incorporation into the presentation. Choose presentation software available on the school computers, or use free web-based applications. Format the presentation to enhance it by showing a process, being persuasive like a movie trailer, or being informational.

Step 4: Present the multimedia presentations to the class. This can be accomplished by using a multimedia presentation, or by creating a channel on websites like Vimeo.

Step 5: Do a presentation about a product. Use all of the available methods known to create and use multimedia presentations (available software, still pictures, motion pictures, etc.).

Select one or more resources from the listing that follows. Research what it can do, and provide a demonstration to the class.

Animoto: an online service that helps create videos from images and video clips.

Blabberize: animate images and make them talk.

Blogspot: allows users to create a simple blog.

Diigo: an online bookmarking service that supports students as they work on a research project.

Edmodo: a resource that provides a way to share classroom content in a way similar to Twitter.

Educreations: tool for sharing video lessons.

GIMP: free photo editing program.

Gliffy: collaborative tool for designing flowcharts and diagrams.

Glogster: an online web service that helps create virtual posters through the use of multimedia.

Google Docs: a word-processing resource to facilitate sharing, creating, and editing documents.

Google Plus: facilitates the use of video chats.

LucidChart: create online diagrams and flowcharts.

Movie: video editing software free on Apple computers.

MyFakeWall: fake Facebook-style profiles for historical figures.

Photovisi: photo collages for downloading and printing.

PicMonkey: photo editing.

Plurk: a social network similar to Twitter.

PowToon: create animated videos and presentations.

Prezi: cloud-based presentation and storytelling tool for presenting ideas on a virtual canvas.

ProConLists: an electronic listing of positives and negatives of an issue.

Queeky: an online drawing tool.

ReadWriteThink: creates cartoons with images and thought bubbles.

Rubistar: an online tool to help design scoring rubrics.

Schoology: a website designed to manage lessons, engage students, and share content.

Shape Collage: facilitates in making an electronic collage.

StudyBlue: online flash cards, quizzes, and study guides for sharing.

Survey Monkey: creates a survey and analyzes the results.

TeacherTube: a video-sharing website designed specifically for classroom use.

Tumblr: an easy tool for blogging.

Twitter: an easy-to-use microblog.

Vimeo: video-sharing website on which users can upload, share, and view videos.

Wall Wisher (padlet): creates a multimedia wall for students to brainstorm ideas, notes, etc.

Webquest: facilitates students as they research content online.

Weebly: a tool for creating a website.

Windows Movie Maker: video editing software on Windows computers.

Wordle: a resource that generates word clouds from text.

YouTube: video-sharing website on which users can upload, share, and view videos.

Unit XVII Summary

Using a variety of electronic resources is a twenty-first-century skill for both teachers and students. Students must be prepared to learn with multimedia as well as be able to demonstrate learning through the same.

Most professions use electronic resources for sharing information, receiving information, or learning. Journalism, engineering, medicine, education, entertainment, and a variety of other commercial industries all use multimedia to produce, advertise, and sell products and services. The challenge for students and educators is not necessarily learning and knowing how to use these resources; rather, the challenge will be to stay up to date with what is available, most useful, and trending.

Technology Adaptation

N/A

POSTTEST

Directions for the Study Skills Posttest

After completing the units in this program, what have you learned and what habits have you modified? Please complete the survey that follows, and explain the benefit of each study habit. Compare this survey to the one you completed at the beginning of the program.

Study Skills Survey

	Always	Sometimes	Never
I review my assignments every day. Benefit: _____ _____ _____ _____			
I try to study in a quiet place. Benefit: _____ _____ _____ _____			

	Always	Sometimes	Never
When necessary, I ask for help. Benefit: _____ _____ _____ _____ _____			
I keep a folder for each subject. Benefit: _____ _____ _____ _____			
I keep my folders organized. Benefit: _____ _____ _____ _____			
I write sample test questions and answer the questions. Benefit: _____ _____ _____ _____			

	Always	Sometimes	Never
I do my homework as early in the day as possible. Benefit: _____ _____ _____ _____			
I keep a "to-do" list of assignments. Benefit: _____ _____ _____ _____			
I turn in all assignments on time. Benefit: _____ _____ _____			
When I take notes, I always write a summary from my notes of what I learned. Benefit: _____ _____ _____			

	Always	Sometimes	Never
I begin studying for tests several days in advance of the exam. Benefit: _____ _____ _____ _____ _____			
I compare my notes to a classmate's notes. Benefit: _____ _____ _____ _____			
I take written notes over text material. Benefit: _____ _____ _____ _____			
I look at bold print, italics, the writing in margins, and study questions before I begin a reading assignment. Benefit: _____ _____ _____ _____			

	Always	Sometimes	Never
I ask the teacher to explain things when I'm confused. Benefit: _____ _____ _____ _____			
When learning new information, I read the text slowly. Benefit: _____ _____ _____ _____			
When I have several homework assignments, I finish the hardest ones first. Benefit: _____ _____ _____ _____			

	Always	Sometimes	Never
When I sit down to study, I have all my supplies organized and ready to use—paper, pencils, computer, etc. Benefit: _____ _____ _____ _____ _____ _____			